Numbers 23:19

Tony L. Hayes

Numbers 23:19

ISBN 978-0-578-53716-0

Library of Congress Control Number: 2019909060

I dedicate this book to:

I dedicate this book to my grandmother Grace, who died in 1995. You told me to put God first, and that He had a plan for my life. I have held on to too what you said Grandma, and God is performing His promises in my life. I know without a doubt that God is a promise keeper. Thank you for inspiring me, and I will let the world know God cannot lie. He will bring to pass just what He has spoken in our lives no matter the obstacles. Grandma, I have learned that God is faithful!

I dedicate this book to my wife, Deborah Hayes and my children Makayla, Elisha, Faith, and Jerome. I dedicate this book to my parents Jerry and Veronica Hayes. I also dedicate this book to my siblings Tanya, Mark, Jerry, and Michael. Finally, I dedicate this book to all my nieces and nephews. I pray that God continues to bless, protect, and His salvation be in our family.

God has so much more for us, hold on to His promises!

Acknowledgments

I want to thank my spiritual father in the Gospel, Bishop Gilbert Robeson. Thank you also, Lady Sheila Robeson. I also want to say grace and peace to Deliverance Cathedral Holiness Church in Burlington, N.C. for supporting my ministry down through the years. Bishop Robeson, thank you again for believing in me and sending me out to labor in God's vineyard.

I am so excited to say thank you Jabez Christian Center in Greensboro, NC. Thank you, everyone, for believing in me and supporting me as your Pastor! The best is yet to come.

I look forward to making an impact with you in ministry on our families, and in the community. God is bringing expansion, and I can't wait to see it in the church. God bless you, and I love you all. I also want to thank Rachel Eggleston for designing my book cover and helping me through this process. God bless you!

Table of Contents

Introduction 1

Chapter 1 Bad hand 4

Chapter 2 Good hand..9

Chapter 3 Renege 20

Chapter 4 Cut it.. 27

Chapter 5 Can anything good come from the hood. 36

Chapter 6 It's not how you start but how you finish.................. 42

Chapter 7 God's hand.. 50

Chapter 8 Caught up in the game 59

Chapter 9 One night 64

Chapter 10 Enough is enough... 70

Chapter 11 A way of escape.. 77

Chapter 12 The mission 84

Chapter 13 There's a war going on....................................... 89

Chapter 14 Poison... 97

Chapter 15 Step up to the challenge.................................... 103

Chapter 16 Spiritually ashy.. 113

Chapter 17 The Lord desires to use you................................ 120

Chapter 18 Let God rebuild your life.................................... 133

Chapter 20 Keep your confidence in the Lord......................... 155

About the author.. 166

Introduction

It's the summer of nineteen ninety-five, and I was lying on my squeaky bed looking up at the ceiling. I'm mumbling a gangster rap song, and I got things on my mind. I'm in too deep, and I got beef with a cat from the streets. The house phone rang, and my pops answered it. I knew something wasn't right about that ring. I could sense it; my grandmother had been in the hospital sick. She had an infection in her blood. My mom calls from the hospital to tell us that her mom and my grandmother had died.

I tried to hold back the tears. I got my beer and blunts that I was hiding in my closet. I hid those things because my parents didn't want that stuff in their house. Tears started streaming down my cheek. I put my beer in one of my pants pockets and went outside to the back porch. I didn't want my dad to see it. When I got outside, I reached into my other pocket and pulled out the blunt that I had rolled up earlier that day.

I flicked the lighter, the fire sparked, and I placed the tail end of the blunt above the fire. It was burning, I inhaled looked up to heaven, and said, "Grandma, I'm going to miss you." I thought rest easy you fought hard for seven years a stroke victim. My mother took care of you. I witness two strong black women who believed in God. It's a hard act to follow growing up in the hood.

I remember before my grandmother Grace died; she told me God was going to do great things in my life. I held on to what she said. I look back on it now and realize God was using her to tell me something. God was going to do something great work in me, and I had no clue at that time. I've come to realize when God makes a promise, He will bring it to pass!

I think back on that day, my grandmother died, and I was taking puffs and choking. Man, that weed was some strong stuff. I recall I coughed and looked up to heaven, and I remember I asked God some questions. I didn't know any better. I said, "God if you love us, why do we struggle so much"? Why did my grandmother die? Why do we live so poor? Why is the hood so messed up, ran down, but the white part of town looks three times better? Why did we get a bad hand?

I inhaled again and blew out the smoke. God if you real please have mercy on me. I was ready to shoot this cat I didn't like. God, I don't want to die or go to jail! Where are you, God? I see my grandparents and parents praying, going to church, but we in the struggle. Where are you, God? It must be a better way. God, do you love us? God, do you love me? God, do you hear me? God, do you love the people from the hood? Are you going to use me? Will I overcome all the pain? I didn't understand back then, but now I know. I understand the scripture numbers twenty-three nineteen!

Let's get it as we start this journey in this book. I hope to inspire, mentor, enrich the youth, the hood, the streets, urban America, and all walks of life, that God can not lie. Life can sometimes deal us a bad hand. However, God never lies, and he will perform His precious promises in our lives. The Lord trumps everybody, even the devil, the joker. God will finish what He started and bring to fruition what He promised His people. God does not renege on what He has spoken concerning us. You can bank on what God promised you! Don't let the enemy fool you with his bluff of deceit.

Chapter 1 Bad hand

You know life can be like a game of cards, and a lot of people from the hood or urban America have received a bad hand. It's not to make an excuse, but it's true looking at it from a spiritual perspective. Let's be honest sometimes its hard understanding that God loves you and has invested so much good in you when you see a lot of negativity. Some may even question can anything good come from my life? The answer is yes if you don't let the devil play you with his bad hands.

Oppression and economic disparity have brought many bad hands. The years of slavery affected the black community and the mental state of blacks. I could only imagine that many slaves probably felt like if God loved us, why we were enslaved and treated like animals? Honestly, I don't have the answer to why God allowed it; but I know He sent His Son Jesus to die for the bad hand or the bad deal. God has made a promise to help us if we turn to Him in our lives.

Today those same questions still can be heard in the hood, because there is still so much economic disparity in the United States. There is still so much police brutality against black males at an alarming rate. Prison systems continue to be filled, with so many young black men. Why God has allowed these things to be, it remains a mystery? I have come to understand through experience that God can use problems, tuff situations, afflictions, disappointments, setbacks, oppression, and sickness like a compass. He can use those things to get us looking and moving in His direction.

I remember growing up in the projects in Greensboro, North Carolina, and I knew our family was dealt a bad hand like so many others. My family struggled so much, financially, that we would receive food assistance. I remember eating the blocks of welfare cheese and making grilled cheese sandwiches. We were so happy because it was good, especially with butter. One day, while I was making a grill cheese sandwich, a movie about Martin Luther King Jr. came on. The movie was so powerful that it changed my life.

I watched that movie and focused on what Martin Luther King Jr. did. He and so many other blacks received a bad hand. They inspired me to want to do great things for myself, family, and the community. I knew I could dream big despite the bad hand.

One thing is for sure life can be unfair. However, it's what you do with the bad hands of life. You can choose to let it inspire you for greatness or bitterness. The welfare cheese memories inspired and pushed our family to God. It motivated us to want more out of life. Poverty motivated me to dream big and never give up. I can't lie my life has had some bad moments because of the bad hand.

However, I humbled myself when God was calling me through the bad hand. It worked for my good. When we humble ourselves under the mighty hand of God, He will lift us. He will bring to pass awesome blessings in our lives. God is faithful, and He cannot lie!

When we allow God to be our compass through the bad hands and deals of life; He can make us more than conquerors. God may allow the bad hand, but at some point, if you follow Him, He knows how to turn it around. God knows how to give us good hands, or should I say blessings!

When I was young, I use to play spades with my friends from the hood. Sometimes I was dealt a bad hand. The hand dealt might have given me a couple of spades because someone was cheating at the table. The hand could have been bad because my partner cut it wrong before we received the cards. When you grow up in the hood, it can feel like life has cheated you. I want to encourage you that God is in the hood. He knows you became frustrated because of the bad hand. However, God is a redeemer.

I used to play spades with some of my friends, consisting of Big P, Teddy, and others. I didn't realize at that time that God would bless us as He has. We received some bad hands when we grew up. We all grew up in the hood, and our families struggled. We lost people to the streets. We all had days when we had to shed tears. However, because of our faith in God through the years, we didn't let those bad hands stop us. It might have slowed us down, but God came through for us.

We learned that God was and is a promise keeper. I remember Big P use to sit at the card table when we were young and say, "Man, I'm going to have my own business and be successful." We would joke with him and be like, "man shut up pass the blunt." God dealt him some good hands down through the years, after bad hands. Big P now has his own trucking company and making six figures. He got several trucks now and he is hiring other drivers.

Oh, I cannot forget about Teddy. Teddy is doing his thing too. My spade partner from back in the day; he is holding it down! I didn't see the big picture back then that my partner would become a successful businessman. He has his own insurance and financial planning business. Teddy was always smart, though, when I think about it. A business mentality was always in him. Our neighborhood would cop the weed from him. He just knew how to make his money. God changed Teddy and showed him how to do it the legal way. I'm so proud of them. People thought we would never make it out the hood, and do great things, but God had other plans. You can't tell me God won't turn things around.

You may start smoking, drinking, and gang banging, or living the street life. God knows you're looking for love because your dad wasn't there. God knows you got a bad hand because of abuse. God knows you got a bad hand called poverty. However, God is allowing the bad hand to get you to see Him in it. He is in it with you, but you must recognize that. It takes patience, understanding, and trust to know that God is with you. You must hang in there!

There were times I got a bad hand in the card game, but I played it out to the end. Bad hands taught me not to give up in the game. We cannot afford to give up in this game called life either. We must play it to the end with the Lord. Card games taught me a lot. Sometimes you could set the other team at the end with face cards; because they over bided their hand.

Sometimes they used their spades too early and didn't have any at the end. They were set and proved wrong. God will trump the devil if you give it to Him; you will prove the devil wrong in the end through Christ. Life can be like a game of cards bad hand, bad deal, but call on Christ. He has mad skills to lift you out of the pit. God has a way of raising us to a place of honor that is where we will sit! Don't give up because God has plans for you! God is in the hood looking for you to answer the call of your divine purpose. God has promises for you, and therefore the enemy is fighting you so hard. God has some good hands on the way! We must hold onto God, and what He said in numbers twenty-three and nineteen!

Chapter 2 Good hand

There is nothing like getting a good hand when you play spades; a good hand when you have had a bad hand before it. A good hand starts to encourage you that you can do something to win the game. A good hand encourages you that you can help your partner in a spade game. A good hand will build up your confidence because you want to carry your weight in the game. You want a good hand so that you can talk some smack to the other team.

Sometimes in life, we need God to turn things around for us, when we have received a bad hand. We can't throw the tile in when we get a bad hand but keep living in life. Quitters never win, and winners never quit! All we need is a good hand from God that includes His grace, goodness, and mercy. A good hand from God that will trump the big joker the devil!

I recall playing spades one night with friends. My partner and I were losing badly. The first few hands dealt were horrible for us. The other team was talking smack as they smoked and got high. They just knew they had the game in the bag. We were still close enough to win.

Things began to change when we started getting good hands. They started getting nervous and started to get quiet. I could sense victory. I told the other team them blunts want help you win tonight. I remember I erupted in laughter.

We were about to win. I could sense the shifting, and of course, the other team didn't like my comment. The other team was upset up now. Things got quiet in the room, and you could hear a pin drop. The game was intense because no one wanted to lose. We came back, but time was running out.

The game was almost over. The other team was slightly ahead when the last hand started. The other team was in a great position. It appeared the other team would hold on for the victory. The only way we could win was with good hands and set the other team. The other team thought they had it and started to talk trash again. All they needed was to get four books on the last hand. It didn't work out for them!

My partner gave out the cards, so it was the other team's time to tell us what they were bidding. I remember them looking at each other and saying, "man, I don't have nothing." I busted out laughing, and so did my partner. We knew we had a chance maybe to set them and win the game. One of the other guys from the other team said to his partner, "man I might be able to get you one that's it." I erupted in laughter again and looked at his partner and said, "How many you got." He said, "shut up, Tony." I knew then we had them. He said, "Man, I might get you one."

We laughed so hard, and they were upset now. My partner and I both had great hands, and we knew they didn't have a lot of spades. My partner called me by my nickname said, "Dog, let's set them and win this game." I said, "for sure homey." My partner said, "so I got six for sure." I started laughing again! I said, "Man, I got five for sure." We looked at each other and laughed! My partner said, "Put us down for eleven books."

The other team started playing their hand, and they thought their ace of hearts would walk. I slammed down my spade on the table because I had no hearts. You could hear the card hitting the table. The sound of victory and I said, "Didn't I tell you that we were going to win." I didn't get an answer from the other team. We clowned them badly on that last hand. We came back and won by setting them on the last hand. Wow, that's what good hands will do for you in spades.

I've learned that God can give you good hands after receiving bad hands. The key is to have a relationship with God because He will fight for you. He will be there when no one else is. He shows up at the appointed time to give His people favor by His hand. When we give our bad hands to God; He can give us good hands by His hand. God will give us blessings because He is a restorer if you let Him.

People may count you out, but God will count you right back in. People may give up on you, but God wants you to too keep pushing. When God has a plan and purpose for your life, no one can stop that. You might have some setbacks in the process. You might feel like you got knocked down by the devil, but God will lift you, and give you victory. You may feel misunderstood, rejected, ostracized, and lied on, but don't quit because God has a reward for you. God has a great hand of blessing. Sometimes bad things happen, but God can perform miracles and bring good out of it.

The Bibles lets us know that some people stoned the Apostle Paul to death. They thought he was dead, but Paul got back up and kept preaching. It's people out there, who have written you off. Your doubters think nothing good will come out of your life. Watch God lift you for His glory and shut the mouths of doubters and liars. We serve a powerful God that's able to do great things in our life. Don't give up but keep doing what God told you to do. He will come through and make the enemy look stupid and shameful. God knows how to give you a good hand! He is a promise keeper.

Acts 14:19-22

19 And there came thither certain Jews from Antioch and Iconium, who persuaded the people, and having stoned Paul, drew him out of the city, supposing he had been dead.20 Howbeit, as the disciples stood round about him, he rose up, and came into the city: and the next day he departed with Barnabas to Derbe.21 And when they had preached the gospel to that city, and had taught many, they returned again to Lystra, and to Iconium, and Antioch,22 Confirming the souls of the disciples, and exhorting them to continue in the faith, and that we must through much tribulation enter into the kingdom of God.

Paul experiences a bad hand in this text. One might even say, "How could God get glory out of this"? How, could God work some good out of this situation? Paul didn't do anything to the people that attacked him. He preached the Gospel, and it made people angry towards him and other believers in the text. He was doing what was right but suffered for it mightily.

Sometimes we're doing the right thing, but bad things happen. Sometimes you may not be bothering anybody, but someone will attack you. People may want to get rid of you, but if God says, "not so." It is nothing they can do about it. God decides when he will call his people home. God has the final say over death.

Here in the text, we have Paul and Barnabas at the start of Acts the fourteenth chapter. God was using them in a profound and mighty way because lives were changed. People were receiving salvation. Paul was also planting churches. Gentiles and some

Jews were being saved and believing in Christ through Paul and Barnabas ministries.

However, unbelieving Jews got jealous and began to stir up trouble and strife while God using Paul, Barnabas, and the disciples. We must understand when true ministry is going forth, and lives are changed, the devil hates it. The devil hates when God is using you. The devil hates when God is restoring you. The devil hates when you get an understanding of who you are in God. He hates it when you and I understand that we're valuable to God. He hates it when God is turning things around in your life. He hates it when God starts giving you good hands.

The devil is jealous of you because he knows God is going to bless you. The enemy uses people to work his jealousy and envy. We must be mature and know that he is trying to get us to act out of character. We must understand his traps and not fall into them. We are not fighting against people but spiritual wickedness. Spiritual wickedness that doesn't want to see you receive the goodness of the Lord!

Ephesians 6:10-13

10 Finally, my brethren, be strong in the Lord, and in the power of his might.11 Put on the whole armor of God, that ye may be able to stand against the wiles of the devil.12 For we wrestle not against flesh and blood, but against principalities, against powers, against the rulers of the darkness of this world, against spiritual wickedness in high places.13 Wherefore take unto you the whole armor of God, that ye may be able to withstand in the evil day, and having done all, to stand.

Sometimes we want to give up and throw in the towel when the struggle comes. Sometimes we want to give up when opposition comes. You're doing the right thing, but all hell breaks loose in your life, and you were trying to do the right thing. We want to throw in the towel when we feel misunderstood. Don't give up because a good hand is coming. We must stay in the press!

Philippians 3:13-14

13 Brethren, I count not myself to have apprehended: but this one thing I do, forgetting those things which are behind, and reaching forth unto those things which are before,14 I press toward the mark for the prize of the high calling of God in Christ Jesus.

Paul said, "I press toward the mark for the prize of the high calling of God in Christ Jesus." We must stay focus and watch God flow in our lives. He has a prize for us in this life and that which is to come. We get to know God when He has us in the press. The press has a way of making you depend and trust Him for the outcome.

Paul and Barnabas were doing the right thing but got mistreated because of it. They were preaching and teaching in Iconium at the beginning of chapter fourteen. Gentiles and some Jews mistreated them. They were planning to kill them. Paul and the disciples found out about it and left Iconium. They were smart to do this at that point. However, the enemy was so jealous and wanted to kill Paul. The apostle thought leaving Iconium would be enough. However, they were determined to stop him. When God starts using you and blessing you with good hands, watch how the jealousy comes.

Paul and the disciples and went into other cities, consisting of Lystra and Derbe to get away from the evil chaos. There they began to preach the Gospel. It appears that God uses the persecution to push Paul, Barnabas, and the disciples to keep going. The kingdom of God grew because more cities were hearing the Word of the Lord. God will use our mistreatment to bring about even more expansion in our life if we would surrender to his will. It is at Lystra that Paul heals a disabled person, and he never laid hands on him.

Acts 14:8-10

8 And there sat a certain man at Lystra, impotent in his feet, being a cripple from his mother's womb, who never had walked:9 The same heard Paul speak: who steadfastly beholding him, and perceiving that he had faith to be healed,10 Said with a loud voice, Stand upright on thy feet. And he leaped and walked.

The cripple man had faith. He wanted to heal from the disease. I want to encourage someone reading this book. Do not be crippled by your situation but have faith to be healed. I know you have been through a lot, but that is not how your story will end. Spiritually tell yourself it is time to get up and walk. It is time to overcome your past. It is time to defeat abuse by standing up and living your life again. God has a good hand waiting for you!

Do not be crippled by your situation but have faith. The man had a disability since birth, but the Word said he had faith to receive healing, and he heard Paul speaking. What was Paul speaking? Paul was preaching the Gospel. The Word of God is life changing and brings healing.

Romans 10:15-17

15 And how shall they preach, except they be sent? As it is written, how beautiful are the feet of them that preach the gospel of peace and bring glad tidings of good things! 16 But they have not all obeyed the gospel. For Esaias saith, Lord, who hath believed our report?17 So then faith cometh by hearing, and hearing by the word of God.

Paul spoke one word, and that was stand; he stood and received healing. My brother, my sister, when you stand, healing is coming in your life. We must stand at some point, rather than continue to have pity parties. We have to stand instead of walking around mad at the world and feeling rejected. It is time to stand because God loves you. He is going to blow your mind when you start standing up for yourself and believing in Him. It may feel like a huge setback, but it was a divine set up for the power of God to be displayed.

The cripple man got up and leaped. He listened to what Paul told him to do. God can perform miracles or bless us if we stand. The man received healing, and then something happens after that. Some of the people misunderstood what had happened; began to say the gods have come down to us.

There were people in the crowd who did not believe in the Lord but believed in false gods such as Zeus and Hermes. They began to do crazy stuff. They had a false priest that believed in these fake gods such as Jupiter, Zeus, Hermes, and other false Greek gods.

Acts 14:11-19

11 And when the people saw what Paul had done, they lifted up their voices, saying in the speech of Lycaonia, The gods are

come down to us in the likeness of men.12 And they called Barnabas, Jupiter; and Paul, Mercurius, because he was the chief speaker.13 Then the priest of Jupiter, which was before their city, brought oxen and garlands unto the gates, and would have done sacrifice with the people.14 Which when the apostles, Barnabas and Paul, heard of, they rent their clothes, and ran in among the people, crying out,15 And saying, Sirs, why do ye these things? We also are men of like passions with you, and preach unto you that ye should turn from these vanities unto the living God, which made heaven, and earth, and the sea, and all things that are therein:16 Who in times past suffered all nations to walk in their own ways.17 Nevertheless he left not himself without witness, in that he did good, and gave us rain from heaven, and fruitful seasons, filling our hearts with food and gladness.18 And with these sayings scarce restrained they the people, that they had not done sacrifice unto them.19 And there came thither certain Jews from Antioch and Iconium, who persuaded the people, and having stoned Paul, drew him out of the city, supposing he had been dead.

Paul and Barnabas said, "Do not worship us." They were not gods. You should not do these things, but they could not stop the crowd because trouble had already started. Verse nineteen said, "And there came thither certain Jews from Antioch and Iconium, who persuaded the people, and having stoned Paul, drew him out of the city, supposing he had been dead."

The same Jews that gave Paul problems in Iconium had now come to where they were at in Lystra. They had walked roughly around a hundred miles to stop the ministry of Paul and Barnabas. People will go out of their way to stop you, but it will not work.

A hundred miles was a long way to walk back then because there were no cars, and most people didn't have horses.

When people go out of their way to stop, you know that God must have great things in store for you! God is going to do awesome things, and the enemy wants to stop it, but he can't. When you see opposition know that your redemption, blessings, and favor is near. I would go ahead and start preparing for a bright future.

Isaiah 46:9-10

9 Remember the former things of old: for I am God, and there is none else; I am God, and there is none like me,10 Declaring the end from the beginning, and from ancient times the things that are not yet done, saying, My counsel shall stand, and I will do all my pleasure:

Nobody can stop God and His counsel; His plans will always prevail. They stoned Paul to death, so they thought, but he was not dead. Notice they took him out of the city and left him for dead. The disciple gathered around Paul, thinking he was dead. I want to encourage someone. People have counted you out, but God has counted you right back in with His mighty hand. God deserves praise for what He is about to do in your life. It is not over to God, say it's over. You're not dead yet, and God has plans for you!

Do not quit because God is confirming what He is about to do in your life. Paul did something in the text concerning confirmation. Paul went back to where they stoned him. Paul went back to the cities that had hurt him. Why would he go back to where people had tried to kill him? Paul went back because he had started something. He had planted churches. He had a vision, and he truly cared for the people that received salvation. He wanted to see these people, and the churches continue to grow in the knowledge of Jesus Christ. He went back to confirm how they were doing.

I want you to tell yourself to go back. You're probably saying go back to what? You can go back to the vision. You can go back to the dream. You can go back to school. You can go back to your family. You can go back to what you have already invested in because God is bringing a harvest into your life. Souls are going to be affected and saved if you go back. Your life is going to change if you go back and pick up the pieces. God knows how to restore your finances if you go back. God knows how to restore things if you go back. God's hand is going to give you a good hand! God cannot lie; let me tell you why. It is numbers twenty-three and nineteen!

Chapter 3 Renege

The word renege has a couple of definition. It can mean as to go back on a promise or contract. It also can mean to play a card that is not of the suit led, when one can follow suit; break a rule of play. When I was growing up in the hood, we played a card game called Spades. I remember I would meet up at someone's house and play. I recall the clouds of smoke that would be in the room and the noise of beer bottles. It was like a quick get away from the stress and situations of life. I enjoyed playing spades.

We played with excitement and with rules. There were several rules to the game. One rule I remember, that is still very important to the game, its call reneging. Reneging was when you had a card of a suit, but you didn't play it when you were supposed to. If you reneged it cost you and your partner books, and points deducted.

Most of the time, when someone reneged, it was because that person was cheating, lying, or operating in deception. One thing I have learned in life is that people lie or walk in deception. However, God doesn't act like people. He is different. God does not lie or operate in deception. We can count on God. He is faithful and true.

Has anyone ever told you they were going to do something for you, but they didn't? They didn't keep their word. The situation may have made you upset, disappointed, or betrayed. My friends, God does not do that to His people. God's Word is true. He performs or will perform all His precious promises to us. It is awesome to know that the God we serve is a promise keeper. People will fail you, but God never fails.

We may not agree with His plans, but He knows what is best for us. God is dependable, and He never lets us down. We can sleep at night knowing God is true to His Word, and He loves us. He has everything under control.

There have been times in my life that I have lied too, and it made me upset. I have learned to put my trust in God and to pray about situations. The Word of God declares we should acknowledge Him in all our doings, and this can help us from being disappointed by people. When we pray and ask God for direction, this can help us from being deceived too often. God will not lie to us, though. When He speaks something over your life, He will bring it to pass. He will not renege on His promises. There is no reneging in Christ.

The Word declares that God cannot lie. It is not a part of who He is. He is a holy God that does not lie. He is trustworthy. We must understand no matter what is happening in our lives, or this world, God's Word will always be true. Let us look at the evidence in God's Word, that He is trustworthy, and there is no lying in Him.

Numbers 23: 19

19 God is not a man, that he should lie; neither the son of man, that he should repent: hath he said, and shall he not do it? or hath he spoken, and shall he not make it good?

The scripture is saying God is not like a man in the sense that He never lies. He won't speak that He is going to do something, and then don't do it. He will make it good. We can take it to the bank. A check or promises from God doesn't bounce. Heaven has no insufficient funds. Heaven doesn't go through recessions or setbacks. We can count on Him with confidence, that the Lord has our backs. God deserves praise, and He will not let us down.

My brothers, my sisters, start preparing for what God has spoken over your life. Let Him walk you through your process for what He has promised. It's yours, and nobody can stop God. Things may happen along the way, but when the dust clears, you will inherit what God promised you.

Isaiah 54:17

17 No weapon that is formed against thee shall prosper, and every tongue that shall rise against thee in judgment thou shalt condemn. This is the heritage of the servants of the Lord, and their righteousness is of me, saith the Lord.

What an encouraging scripture the Word gives us. When weapons form that could take us out, or destroy the promises of God in our life, God stops it. The weapon or threat does not prosper. When people run their mouth in judgment against you, God has a way of correcting them. God has a way of stopping the liar, and there lies. God has a way of stopping the person who speaks evil against you. Their mouths and evil intentions will not prosper when the dust clears.

No matter who wants to curse you or try and stop the plan, that God has for your life, they cannot. We must stay focus and stand on the promises of God knowing He is a promise keeper. He will not lie. He will perform just what He said. The prophet Jeremiah learned this about God as well.

Jeremiah 1:11-12

11. Moreover the word of the Lord came unto me, saying, Jeremiah, what seest thou? And I said, I see a rod of an almond

tree.12 Then said the Lord unto me, Thou hast well seen: for I will hasten my word to perform it.

The scripture encourages us that God will perform His Word. The Lord asked Jeremiah a question. He said, "What do you see"? Before God said, "I'm going to perform it." He said, "What do you see"? We must see it through the eyes of faith, that God is going to work everything out for us that He promised. Can you see it? Can you see yourself in a better situation? Can you see yourself blessed and favored by God? Can you see yourself prospering and being successful for God? Can you see yourself being a blessing to others as God blesses you? Can you see it?

We must see it in the spiritual realm, because the natural realm may be saying something contrary to what God has spoken. There is the reason why the Bible tells us to walk by faith, not by sight. I'm talking about natural sight, not spiritual sight. When we walk by spiritual sight, we can see through the eyes of faith that God will not renege on His promises.

No one can curse you when God has already declared you blessed. Don't let anyone trick you out of God's blessing. Don't ever let someone make you feel like you're not blessed. You're blessed, so keeping walking with the Lord. People will try to curse you because they see that you're blessed. They know God is going to give you victory after victory. Sometimes people will go out of their way to stop you, but it will not work. The Word of God encourages us again!

Numbers 23:20-24

20 Behold, I have received commandment to bless: and he hath blessed; and I cannot reverse it.21 He hath not beheld iniquity in Jacob, neither hath he seen perverseness in Israel: the

LORD his God is with him, and the shout of a king is among them.22 God brought them out of Egypt; he hath as it were the strength of an unicorn.23 Surely there is no enchantment against Jacob, neither is there any divination against Israel: according to this time it shall be said of Jacob and of Israel, What hath God wrought!24 Behold, the people shall rise up as a great lion, and lift up himself as a young lion: he shall not lie down until he eat of the prey, and drink the blood of the slain.

These scriptures let us know that no one can reverse what God has declared, and he will do it. No one can stop God's plan. It doesn't matter how much evil someone conjures up in their heart. It will not work. Witchcraft and working evil will not prevail against what God has spoken.

Let me give you a quick summary of this text. There are two men in this story in Numbers twenty-third chapter. God is dealing with Balaam and Balak. These two men want to curse the Lord's people, the Israelites. God had made a promise to his servant Abraham that His people would possess the land and become a great nation.

However, God told Abraham that His people would go into bondage for four hundred years. He promised to bring them out, and He did. There is no reneging in His promises. God raised Moses to be His servant to help lead the Israelites from Egypt. God led His people out of Egypt and performed great miracles. The people, however, still did not believe.

They cross the Red Sea. The people murmured and complained against God and Moses. However, in Numbers twenty-one, the Israelites began to fight the other nations for their promise. They were moving towards the promise, and then they had to fight other nations on their way to their promise. I need to ask a question. Are you still spiritually fighting for what God said was yours? Are you still believing and trusting God for the promise?

The Israelites started fighting the other nations. They were kicking some tail because God was with them. They were winning, and the other nations were scared. It was in their hearts that the Israelites were coming to defeat them. Numbers the twenty-second chapter Balak sees the Israelites coming and is scared. He figures I have to do something to stop them. He believes that if I curse them, and work some magic on them, I can stop them. He did not understand that God had made a promise to His people. Balak found out the hard way that God can not lie. He was not able to prevail over God's people. He could not curse them!

Hebrews 6: 13-18

13.For when God made a promise to Abraham, because he could swear by no greater, he sware by himself,14 Saying, Surely blessing I will bless thee, and multiplying I will multiply thee.15 And so, after he had patiently endured, he obtained the promise.16 For men verily swear by the greater: and an oath for confirmation is to them an end of all strife.17 Wherein God, willing more abundantly to shew unto the heirs of promise the immutability of his counsel, confirmed it by an oath:18 That by two immutable things, in which it was impossible for God to lie, we might have a strong consolation, who have fled for refuge to lay hold upon the hope set before us.

God told Abraham surely, I will bless and multiply you. God was saying you can rely or bank on it. It will come to pass. Did Abraham go through something during that time? The answer is yes. The scripture stated that he patiently endured, and this is how he obtained the promises. I am learning that when God makes a promise to me; I must be patient as He brings it to pass. It's not always easy, but I have learned it is worth the wait!

God is up to something in our lives. He has plans for us, and He will not disappoint. No need to worry if He will do it, it is already done! It will happen, and there is no reneging in God because of numbers twenty-three and nineteen.

Chapter 4 Cut it

Years ago, card games taught me some things about life. What I mean by that is someone would deal you cards, and you had no control in what you received. We don't get to control what life brings sometimes. Sometimes it's good, and sometimes it's bad. Spades taught me to be watchful because you had to watch the table.

Honestly back then I don't know how focus I was, with all the smoke and drinking going on. However, I tried to watch the table, especially the opposing team. It was something about those games when we played spades. Whenever we cut books, we would slam the cards down. It was fun for me to cut somebody's book when they thought they had it. The other team clowned me as well when they took my book or my teammate's.

Those cards game would cause us to start talking junk to the other team as well, and of course, they talked smack back. Well, while all the talking smack, you had to watch the table. You had to watch because the person shuffling the cards; if they were good, they could leave good cards for themselves or their partner. The way to combat that was to cut it. You had to know how to cut it the right way.

One of my homeboys was good at shuffling, and he knew how to leave the Big Joker on the bottom. You had to cut it if you didn't, he would end up with the most powerful card on the table. The thing about cutting it was an option if it was your turn to cut. We have an option in life to cut stuff. You can cut stuff that's not conducive to the plan and purpose that God has for your life. I am not talking about a physical cutting but a spiritual one. We must know when to cut it.

You may be saying cut what? You must cut things out of your life that is toxic. There may be things that hinder the process that God is orchestrating in your life. You must cut things off that stop your flow in God. We must learn to cut things off that make us upset all the time. We must know when to cut things off, which hinder our flow. God desires that we flow with Him. It's hard to flow with God, and toxic things are weighing you down. Don't let anything stop your flow or take your flow in God.

God wants us to flow in what He has given us, but also have wisdom. We must protect the flow of God in our life. It is precious! Your relationship with God is precious. Sometimes the cutting involves us. We must get rid of bad habits, or the sin that is hindering us in our life.

Hebrews 12:1-2

12 Wherefore seeing we also are compassed about with so great a cloud of witnesses, let us lay aside every weight, and the sin which doth so easily beset us, and let us run with patience the race that is set before us. 2. Looking unto Jesus the author and finisher of our faith; who for the joy that was set before him endured the cross, despising the shame, and is set down at the right hand of the throne of God.

We keep must keep our eyes on the Savior as we run the race, and He will let us know what to cut. One thing I have learned in my walk with God is to be obedient. When God tells us to cut it, we need to do it, because He knows what is best for us. He knows if we cut it. It will produce a better life for us and better results.

John 15:1-2

15 I am the true vine, and my Father is the husbandman.2 Every branch in me that beareth not fruit he taketh away: and every branch that beareth fruit, he purgeth it, that it may bring forth more fruit.

Sometimes we must cut abusive relationships out of our lives. We must cut it out. God did not put us here on earth to suffer abuse physically or verbally. God has so much more for you. God is a forgiving God. He has the authority to forgive you if you made a mistake in your decision-making. Quit beating yourself up, and cut that toxic relationship, which is causing you to miss out on the life that God has for you. God is about peace and love, not abuse.

I remember playing spades, and sometimes cutting the cards right gave us good hands. When we learn the gift of cut it, watch how some things work out for our good. It doesn't make you a bad person, because you must love and care about yourself. We must love ourselves enough to know when to cut things out of our life. When we don't, it could affect us, our families, and our communities. Don't let the big joker, the devil get you, cut it.

There is a very interesting story in the Bible where a king had to cut some stuff off. Hezekiah, the king learned the gift of cut it. He had to cut or stop some stuff that would have taken him and the people out. We must understand the enemy is a thief. He will attempt to come in and take what God has given you if you don't learn to cut it. We must be able to cut it. Let's look at the Word of God.

2 Chronicles 32:1-8

32 After these things, and the establishment thereof, Sennacherib king of Assyria came, and entered into Judah, and encamped against the fenced cities, and thought to win them for himself.2 And when Hezekiah saw that Sennacherib was come, and that he was purposed to fight against Jerusalem,3 He took counsel with his princes and his mighty men to stop the waters of the fountains which were without the city: and they did help him.4 So there was gathered much people together, who stopped all the fountains, and the brook that ran through the midst of the land, saying, Why should the kings of Assyria come, and find much water?5 Also he strengthened himself, and built up all the wall that was broken, and raised it up to the towers, and another wall without, and repaired Millo in the city of David, and made darts and shields in abundance.6 And he set captains of war over the people, and gathered them together to him in the street of the gate of the city, and spake comfortably to them, saying,7 Be strong and courageous, be not afraid nor dismayed for the king of Assyria, nor for all the multitude that is with him: for there be more with us than with him:8 With him is an arm of flesh; but with us is the Lord our God to help us, and to fight our battles. And the people rested themselves upon the words of Hezekiah king of Judah.

Hezekiah, who is the king in this text, and the people, had come under attack. The wicked king, Sennacherib had come to attack, and take advantage of the people of God. He wanted to talk junk to them, kill them, but drink their water as he did it. However, Hezekiah stood up and said, "Not here you want." There are times when we must learn to stand up for our families, and ourselves and say, "this is going to stop." It's time to cut it. Hezekiah cut it.

If you study Hezekiah, you will find that he had issues. However, he would not allow the enemy to come in and steal. Hezekiah was committed to God. However, just because we are faithful to God, doesn't mean we won't come under attack or go through things. (2 Kings 18:13-16).

When Hezekiah realized that the enemy was going to attack him and the people. The king stopped the flow of the water outside of Jerusalem. We must stop letting the enemy use our blessings, and they don't mean us well, it's time to cut it. I must stress this, protect what God has given you because it is important. Hezekiah and the people not only stopped the water from flowing outside the city, but he began to build walls to protect the people from the enemy. They wanted to guard their city. We must guard our lives, our families, and the community. However, it first starts with us. We must take care of ourselves, which includes our bodies, hearts, and minds.

Proverbs 4:23

23 Keep thy heart with all diligence; for out of it are the issues of life.

We protect our minds by abiding in Him. We protect our mind by staying in the Word of God and prayer. We protect our minds by being obedient to the Lord.

1Samuel 15:22

22 And Samuel said, Hath the Lord as great delight in burnt offerings and sacrifices, as in obeying the voice of the Lord? Behold, to obey is better than sacrifice, and to hearken than the fat of rams.

God sees things that we perhaps don't see when He is telling us to cut it. There have been times in my life that I learned the hard way, and I didn't have to. I just needed to obey the Lord. One-time God told me not to do business with a company, but I didn't listen. God was telling me to cut that business relationship because the people were shady. Well, because I didn't listen, it ended up being a bad business decision, and I lost money and my time. I've learned now when God says cut it; I'm cutting it!

We must be prepared for the battle and be courageous when God tells us to cut it. Hezekiah stopped the water from flowing outside, built walls for protection, and gathered the people to fight. Hezekiah used these tactics of preparation against the enemy, and then he encouraged the people to be strong and courageous. Courageous means to have the mental or moral strength to venture, persevere, and withstand danger, fear, or difficulty. (Merriam Webster)

Joshua 1:1-8

1 Now after the death of Moses the servant of the Lord it came to pass, that the Lord spake unto Joshua the son of Nun, Moses' minister, saying,2 Moses my servant is dead; now therefore arise, go over this Jordan, thou, and all this people, unto the land which I do give to them, even to the children of Israel.3 Every place that the sole of your foot shall tread upon, that have I given unto you, as I said unto Moses.4 From the wilderness and this Lebanon even unto the great river, the river Euphrates, all the land of the Hittites, and unto the great sea toward the going down of the sun, shall be your coast.5 There shall not any man be able to

stand before thee all the days of thy life: as I was with Moses, so I will be with thee: I will not fail thee, nor forsake thee.6 Be strong and of a good courage: for unto this people shalt thou divide for an inheritance the land, which I sware unto their fathers to give them.7 Only be thou strong and very courageous, that thou mayest observe to do according to all the law, which Moses my servant commanded thee: turn not from it to the right hand or to the left, that thou mayest prosper withersoever thou goest.8 This book of the law shall not depart out of thy mouth; but thou shalt meditate therein day and night, that thou mayest observe to do

This text in the Bible lets us know we must be courageous when God is flowing in our life. We must realize courageous when God is taking us somewhere in Him. God was taking Joshua and the people into the promised land. A land flowing with milk and honey, God had a better life for them. It was time to cross over into it. Joshua and the people had to be courageous and trust God as they crossed over.

God is going to help us cross over into what He has for us, even though it has been a struggle. I encourage you to cut off anything spiritually that is upsetting you and stopping your progress. I encourage you to take on strength and be strong. I encourage you to keep your confidence in God as you cut some stuff off. Please remember to protect your flow in God by having confidence in Him. Don't throw your confidence because it's going to bring about a reward for you!

Hebrews 10:35-39

35 Cast not away therefore your confidence, which hath great recompense of reward.36 For ye have need of patience, that, after ye have done the will of God, ye might receive the promise.37 For yet a little while, and he that shall come will come, and will not tarry.38 Now the just shall live by faith: but if any man draw back, my soul shall have no pleasure in him.39 But we are not of them who draw back unto perdition; but of them that believe to the saving of the soul.

God has given us something to cut with, sharper than a sword. This weapon is called the Word of God, and this why I share the Word in my books. The Word of God is powerful. It provides comfort, direction, understanding, and is the sharpest weapon against the enemy. It destroys the enemy, and this why the enemy doesn't want us to read the Word of God. The Word of God lets us know that the enemy is already defeated.

The Word of God contains the promises of God, which brings peace, and joy, knowing the Lord is a promise keeper. The Word of God reveals to us what God desires to do in our life. It gives hope and discipline. Who wouldn't want the sharpest weapon out there? The most powerful weapon on earth and a lot of people let their Bibles collect dust. We must use our weapon, the Word of God effectively. The Word of God has a way of revealing to us what we need to cut in our lives.

Hebrews 4:12

12 For the word of God is quick, and powerful, and sharper than any two-edged sword, piercing even to the dividing asunder

of soul and spirit, and the joints and marrow, and is a discerner of the thoughts and intents of the heart.

God is going to give you a good hand if you put it in His hand when He tells you to cut it. There is nothing worth our peace, joy, blessings, and deliverance in God. The Lord is trying to protect you from something. He also is trying to bless you as you cut it, watch the peace come when you let it go!

Chapter 5 Can anything good come from the hood.

I used to wonder what the heart, diamond, club, and spade symbolized on the cards. After doing the research, I found that they symbolize the seasons of our life. We go through four main seasons in our life, consisting of childhood, youth, adult, and old age. However, it was something about the heart. It stood out to me, as a child. I later realized that the heart was significant to me because of its meaning. I later realize that the heart symbolized things like childhood, spring, love, emotions, and vulnerability. Childhood is a time where God starts to develop our spiritual hearts and reveals to us right and wrong. Our hearts develop emotions, and we start to look for love in our childhood days. It was in my childhood where I wonder could anything good come from the hood!

The Word of God said we should train up a child in the way that he should go, and when he is older, he won't depart. I hope to encourage someone to train your child up in the ways of God. God can take a child's spiritual heart and begin to use them at an early age. God doesn't want us to get played by the devil, but it starts in childhood. The devil doesn't want anything good to come from the hood, so he tries to deceive us early on in life. The devil's wish is to mess up a child's mind or heart early, so that they won't be productive and a God-fearing person later.

The highest card in the suit of hearts is the ace. It's the card of desire. One meaning for the word ace in cards is I am. Our hearts should desire the great I am. Jesus is the great I am. When we desire Him, good things can come out of the hood. When we are ready to follow Him, He will show us great things and use us for His glory. God must be our ace, our best friend. The one we desire the most. God can do great things through us if we hunger and thirst after Him.

I must keep it real. Over twenty-five years ago I had questions, smoking weed and playing cards with my homeboys, I didn't understand. I didn't understand that the cards we were using to have fun with were telling us about life. I sometimes wonder while chilling with my peeps if God loved the hood or inner city. Why was it so messed up on our side of town? When I saw a picture of Jesus, He was white, and I thought to myself why? My parents are black, and in the struggle praying to a white God. I saw many people struggling while we were staying in the projects, in the hood.

I saw young black males selling drugs, thinking they were living the life, but they were being set up for failure and death. I saw prostitution. I saw some addicted to drugs. People were fighting and killing each other. I'm thinking to myself at a young age, why are we doing these things? We're the same color. God if your real and you love us, why are things like this? Why did we get a bad hand? I was a child, but I was thinking can anything good come from the hood. The answer is yes!

I remember early one morning standing at the bus stop with my sister. We were little kids. I recall seeing a white van roll slowly by us. A few white men were staring at us. They had the side door to the van open. One of the white men was holding something in his hand. It was a gun. Later, my family and the community learned that the men rolling in that white van were the Ku Klux Klan. Thankfully no harm came to my sister and me, but weeks later, those same men shot a black man not far from where we lived. As a child, that left me with many questions.

I wondered if God loved black people. I wondered if God loved the hood. I wondered if anything good could come out of the mess, which I saw and experienced. I wondered if anything good could come out of my family because we were affected by our environment. I wondered if anything good could come out of me, or would I end up a failure?

I learned through it all that I had to believe in God's promises. I didn't know then, but now I know that God can not lie. When God declares He is going to do something, He will! I look back on it now after God saved me. He gave me new perspectives. I knew something good could come out of the hood. When my relationship with God increased, I knew something good could come out of the environment.

I know this now because God let us know in His Word, that Jesus came out of Nazareth. Jesus came from a despised, rejected, and small city. Nazareth was an obscure city. Some might say it was in the backwoods where no one would expect anything good to come out of it.

The King of Kings comes out of Nazareth. Jesus came from a town that was despised and rejected. History tells us, the people of Nazareth, were looked down upon by some people from Judea. They despised them because of how they talked and how they lived. The people of Nazareth lived very poor and humble lives back then. The surrounding cities thought what good could come out of something like that. The people of Nazareth were trying to survive and live day to day without all the money. Does that sound familiar in black and poor communities in America today?

Often, people look down on people from the hood, inner city, projects, and poor communities. People make assumptions about others based on where they live. Many people may question what good can come out of the hood? Sometimes people who live in the hood may question, can anything good come out of the hood. The answer is Yes! God can raise you up.

God let us know that if He came from dealing with hate, rejection, poverty, and feeling misunderstood, then so can we. He not only came out of it, but He fulfilled His purpose while here on earth. Christ answered the skeptics, the doubters, and the hater's question; which was can anything good come out of Nazareth? The answer was yes because Christ was the good Shepard that would come out of Nazareth.

He would die for the sins of man and reconcile us back to God becoming our Savior. I want to encourage you that God loves the hood. There is a relationship that God desires with people from the hood, and it's always been there. There is something unique about God and the hood. Let us examine some scriptures to enlighten us on our journey to understanding God's love for the hood or the despised.

John 1:43-50

43 The day following Jesus would go forth into Galilee, and findeth Philip, and saith unto him, Follow me.44 Now Philip was

of Bethsaida, the city of Andrew and Peter.45 Philip findeth Nathanael, and saith unto him, We have found him, of whom Moses in the law, and the prophets, did write, Jesus of Nazareth, the son of Joseph.46 And Nathanael said unto him, Can there any good thing come out of Nazareth? Philip saith unto him, Come and see.47 Jesus saw Nathanael coming to him, and saith of him, Behold an Israelite indeed, in whom is no guile!48 Nathanael saith unto him, Whence knowest thou me? Jesus answered and said unto him, Before that Philip called thee, when thou wast under the fig tree, I saw thee.49 Nathanael answered and saith unto him, Rabbi, thou art the Son of God; thou art the King of Israel.50 Jesus answered and said unto him, Because I said unto thee, I saw thee under the fig tree, believest thou? thou shalt see greater than these things.

Nathaniel questioned Phillip, who came and told him about Jesus. He questioned Phillip because he said, "Jesus was from Nazareth.". Can anything good come out of Nazareth? Nathaniel was saying, "how can something good come out of that despised and messed up city." However, God proves Nathaniel's assumptions wrong and forgave him as well. Jesus said unto him, "I saw you under the fig tree before Phillip even came to you." Nathaniel was impressed that Jesus already knew who he was, and he hadn't talked to him yet. At that moment, he was ready to receive Jesus.

Jesus knew that Nathaniel was an Israelite, and he also knew about his character before they met. Nathaniel knew only God could have known such things because he had never met Jesus. Jesus saw the good in Nathaniel, even though he was judging Him. Jesus didn't allow false assumptions to stop his purpose. He tells

Nathaniel in verse fifty, "you're going to see greater things than this."

My brothers and sisters, when people make false assumptions about you, be encouraged and stand strong in Christ. People may try to make you feel insignificant because of your ties to the hood, but your ties to the hood won't stop God from using you in a great way. Whatever God has put in your heart to do for Him, He will bring it to pass. God cannot lie according to the scripture numbers twenty-three and nineteen.

Jesus still sees the good in people even when others make false assumptions. We must be willing to forgive others when they make assumptions that are not true about us. We may come from the hood, but there is some good stuff down on the inside. God is trying to bring the good out of us. Don't fall for the devil's bluff because he's blowing smoke because God has good things, he desires to give to you. I ask you can anything good come from the hood. The answer is yes! Think numbers twenty-three and nineteen!

Chapter 6 It's not how you start but how you finish

The club that we see on a card symbolizes the second phase of life, which is being a youth. It also means summer, mind, intellect, and irresponsibility. Sometimes bad things happen to good people because we make bad decisions in our youth. When you're growing up in tuff environments, it can discourage you, but don't let that be the end of your story.

God can redeem us. God can heal us from hurt and pain. God has allowed some of us to survive traumatic things, which could have taken us out. I know what it is like to get a bad start like so many of us. Like so many others, I didn't grow up in a nice neighborhood. I grew up in the projects, the hood. My homeboys and I had some issues, but we overcame the club stage. For example, my homeboy Big P. Sometimes, I look at Big P's testimony for encouragement. Wow, a testimony from a brother from the hood!

Big P started as a troubled teen, living in the projects and no father. He partied, clubbed, sold dope, and loved the ladies, but that's not how his story ended. One day he began to feel pain in his chest. The pain was so intense that he decided to go to the hospital. During that visit, the doctor explained that he needed to change. He couldn't continue to indulge in smoking or drinking, or it wouldn't end well for him. That was the turning point! He made the wise decision to stop! Remembering what his grandmother taught him, he told me that he got down on his knees and prayed. At that moment, things began to change. Big P took heed to the doctor's advice and started the journey towards becoming healthy. On top of becoming healthy, he started to go to church and found a beautiful wife. He noticed how God was blessing him. You see, Big P was tired of living the life he was living. Just like Big P, God has a plan and purpose for your life; even if it looks dark and gloomy.

God can use people who have been through traumatic things or had a rough life. The Lord can choose a person like that, to do great things in his kingdom. We must change our focus from our bad experiences, to what God can do. God is a healer, physically, emotionally, and mentally. It's not how you start but how you finish. I'm here to tell you just because something bad happened to you doesn't mean God can't turn it around.

God will help us finish strong and become an overcomer of our past. God has a future for us, that is far better than our past. He knows all about our pain; and what we have experienced. God will use our pain to produce something great in our lives. We must learn to let the bitterness go of what has happened to us. God can help us overcome the mistakes and the irresponsibility of our youth.

When I was growing up, I played basketball and baseball. I remember one basketball game. My team had a bad start to one of our conference rivals. We were down halftime by ten points. At halftime, we went into the locker room with our heads hanging down. The coach didn't come in. We sat there for a few minutes, in the locker room, thinking about the game. I remember thinking about some of the bad decisions I had made. Feeling nervous, my coach walks in. He gave the team a good pep talk. He told us we were not playing our game, and he wanted us to settle down and have fun. It was obvious that we were putting too much pressure on ourselves. We took his advice. The team settled down in the second half, started having fun, and playing our game. We made a comeback and beat the other team by fifteen points. During that time, I learned that it wasn't how I started but how I finished.

You see that's what you call a turn-around. God wants to turn it around for you, with a great comeback from all the hurt and pain. It's not over until God says it's over. God knows how to give you a comeback. It's not how you start but how you finish!

In the bible, there's a man by the name of Jabez. God gave him a comeback and a strong finish. Being birthed in pain, he went through some things. However, the struggle did not define him. He didn't let the pain stop him from having a great life in God. Perhaps he went through a lot as a youth, but it appears, with God, he became a certified winner!

God can bring something out of our pain if we don't give up. Jabez didn't give up, and neither should we. It's not how you start, but how you finish. We can learn from Jabez, so let's look at the story of Jabez for a minute.

1 Chronicles 4:9-10

9 And Jabez was more honourable than his brethren: and his mother called his name Jabez, saying, Because I bare him with sorrow.10 And Jabez called on the God of Israel, saying, Oh that thou wouldest bless me indeed, and enlarge my coast, and that

thine hand might be with me, and that thou wouldest keep me from evil, that it may not grieve me and God granted him that which he requested.

There is an old saying that prayer changes things. Jabez had some struggles, but the Bible lets us know that he still became a praying man. Our struggle will lead us to pray if we humble ourselves, and admit to God, I need your help. Jabez humbled himself and prayed.

Philippians 4:6-7

6 Be careful for nothing; but in everything by prayer and supplication with thanksgiving let your requests be made known unto God.7 And the peace of God, which passeth all understanding, shall keep your hearts and minds through Christ Jesus.

Here in this text, the theme of prayer comes to life for Jabez. The text describes the character of this man. It states that "he was more honorable than his brothers." It didn't say he was better, but he was more honorable.

What made him more honorable? The answer is the way he lived his life. Jabez was a man of prayer and a man that had a relationship with God. He was a man that didn't give up, and it appears he didn't have a father in his life. However, it didn't stop him from having a relationship with God. The text implies that this man was influential because of his relationship with God. It didn't start well for him or his mother, but it ended with the blessing of God on his life.

The name Jabez means pain or sorrow in Hebrew. He was given that name by his mother, because of the pain she experienced birthing him. It was a rough start for him and his mother. Jabez didn't allow this to be the end of his story. God can use our pain to birth something great in our life.

We learn that the odds were against Jabez, but he didn't allow his fatherless situation to persuade him to give up. He had a bad hand. Some may grow up without a father. It's a bad start, but the story doesn't have to end there. God will be your father, and he will never abandon you. He loves you and desires full custody of you and not weekend visits. He will support you because you're His child with His DNA!

We, as God's people can't let the pain or the storms of life, get the best of us. It may sometimes seem like life is kicking our butt. I want to encourage someone to begin praying and seeking God in your situation. God has a way of getting us past the pain and helping us to experience healing, blessings, joy, and His peace.

Romans 8:28

28 And we know that all things work together for good to them that love God, to them who are the called according to his purpose.

God will take our setbacks, pain, abuse, hurt, and will give testimonies in the end. He weaves it all together for our good. Our bad experiences can sometimes be used later on to help others; to have compassion. When we love God, He brings things together for our good. The purpose and the plans that He has for our life will happen.

Jabez called upon the God of Israel. He called, or he cried out to God. Our situations and circumstances have a way of making us cry out to God. Don't be ashamed to cry out to God; tell God all about it. He already knows, but sometimes, God wants us to talk to Him. He wants us to pray with sincerity. When we truly understand, who we serve, and realize that He answers prayer. We will spend time with Him. We will get in His Word. We will trust Him and have no doubt. We will cast all our cares upon Him; even when it doesn't make sense to do so.

When we spend time with God, we will learn to pray for the will of God in our life. What we desire for ourselves, and what God desires to give to us are two different things. God knows what is best for us. Jabez realized that the God of Israel always wanted to bless His people. It was in the Word that His people would be blessed. Jabez makes a profound statement after he cried out to God. He said, "Bless me, indeed."

The word indeed means to confirm or agree with something that has already been spoken. Jabez's prayer was I agree with you God; because you have already declared you're going to bless me. We must come to a place in our walk with God, where we agree with what God is saying about us. What is God saying about you?

Jabez wanted what God desired for him. He came into agreement and harmony with God. God answered his request when he came into agreement with Him. When we pray about what God desires for us to have; He will put a desire in us to do his will. Our lives and situations will turn around. Jabez cried out to God, and he asked in detail what he wanted God to do for Him. It started bad, but it changed because of the power of prayer. It changed because he fellowshipped with God. It's not how you start, but how you finish!

God enlarged or expanded Jabez; in other words, He gave him the land. We must understand in the stretching God is going to enlarge or expand us. Sometimes it can feel like God is stretching us, and it's uncomfortable. Stretching is when God is saying keep going; keep pressing toward your goal. When God is stretching us, he will take what little we have and make something great out of it. God can enlarge your money in the stretching. God can bring more peace in the stretching. God can restore you in the stretching. God can bring an increase in our lives if we receive it and trust Him. I believe that God wants to prosper us in every area of our lives.

3 John 1:2 2.

Beloved, I wish above all things that thou mayest prosper and be in health, even as thy soul prospereth.

Jeremiah 29:11-13

11 For I know the thoughts that I think toward you, saith the Lord, thoughts of peace, and not of evil, to give you an expected end.12 Then shall ye call upon me, and ye shall go and pray unto me, and I will hearken unto you.13 And ye shall seek me, and find me when ye shall search for me with all your heart.

Are you ready to walk in a new life? Are you ready for an abundance of peace and joy? Are you ready to walk like a King's kid? Are you ready to walk in your destiny? Are you ready for more? God wants to give us more; do you want it? It's not how you start, but how you finish.

Jabez was ready for more of God even though he had experienced pain. After he asks God to enlarge him, he said, "I want your hand to stay with me." Jabez wanted God's presence in his life. Whenever you have the presence of God in your life; you will see his power operating. God's power can bring healing, grace, mercy, protection, and favor in situations. The power of God turns things around in our lives. Power belongs to God!

Are we using the power that God has put in us? The power to pray that will change us or change our situations. The power to speak those things that be not as though they were! We must learn to speak what God declares about us.

Jabez, then he asks God to keep him from evil or harm. He ends his prayer to God that it might not grieve me. We shouldn't desire something or someone that is going to bring grief in our lives. However, we should desire what God wants for us. God's plan is better than our plan. God has more for us than just pain and struggle. Don't let the enemy trick you because of the sins of your youth or past. Please remember it's not how you start, but how you finish!

Chapter 7 God's hand

Sometimes we must realize that we're like that diamond on that card. We're a diamond in the ruff. The diamond represents the adult stage of life. It symbolizes things like the fall, careers, values, and responsibility. When I look back on things, I can see God's hand moving in my life as I matured into an adult. I could also see great progress in Teddy's life, as well. God did great things in his life by His powerful and unstoppable hand.

God will fight for us with His powerful hands, and I promise you no one stop God. He is undefeated! He is developing you into someone valuable to His kingdom, your family, and the community. We're valuable to God like a diamond. However, we must understand that when we put our lives in His hand, amazing things will happen for us. We must grow up and mature if we hunger for God to do great things in our life.

I remember growing up in the hood. There was a phrase we used concerning fighting, "can you throw those hands." The phrase meant could you fight. You had to know how to fight, throw those hands when you had beef. You had to know how because at some point someone was going to test you. I remember Teddy he was that guy that could throw them hands. However, as he grew up, his faith was tested. It was no longer how good he could fight in the natural but in the spiritual! I must tip my hat to Teddy. I believe he learned to put it in God's hand because the Lord is a promise keeper.

I remember Teddy telling me how he got his life insurance license in 2008. It was a sacrifice for him, but he stepped out on faith because he wanted a better life. He wanted a life free from hustling drugs and beefing with cats. Teddy called me on the phone one day and was like "Tone I got my license, but I don't know how this insurance thing is going to turn out." He was like, "Man, I have never done anything like this, but my cousin told me I could do it." I said, "Man, you can do it." Teddy said, "I have to take these leads and go out and talk to strangers."

I was like, "Teddy we from the streets, if you hustle on the streets than you can do this, man." He was like, "I think your write Tone I'm going to do my best and put the rest in God's hands. Teddy struggled for a few months because of rejection. He received a good measure of being told no by strangers. However, once he started learning how to handle objections and increased his activity in the field. He started making a lot of money. I said, "Man, how did you do it"?

He said, "yo, my boss trained me how to handle to common objections." The two objections were I'm not interested, and I can't afford it. He said, "Tone I heard those two objections all the time." He said, "At first I would just say ok and move on." Teddy, however, learned to counter with I'm not sure if you should be interested. However, if you give me fifteen minutes of your time; I can show you how this service can be beneficial to you.

When he closed, and someone said, "I can't afford it." Teddy's reply would be you can't afford not to, because if you die today would you want your family to suffer; because you don't have life insurance? Do you love your wife and family? Well, guess what most men love their wives and families. Teddy knew if the wife were there, it would work in his favor.

When he learned to counter back, he started getting more appointments and closing more often. He called me on the phone one day was like, "Tone man I'm rolling now." Teddy didn't think he could do it at first, but he blossomed in financial services. He became a great salesman and agency owner. He's making six figures every year and has his block of business. God will put us in a process, and we must trust Him. God has a way of blessing if we stay in our process.

Our natural hands can receive strength from God's hand. The hand of God in our lives ultimately gives us victory. Our hands are limited. Our hands cannot compare to God's. He is a big God that does big things by His hands. God's hand is so enormous He has the whole world in His hand.

David knew this, as well. He knew that he could fight, but it was God who gave the victory. It was God, who showed David how to use his hands in the first place. God made us, and He knows all about us. He knows our weaknesses and limitations. We must learn to put our lives in His hands. We must learn to put situations and circumstances in His hand.

We can put it in God's hand because He knows how to fight for us. He knows how to give us a complete victory. I don't know about you, but I want to have complete victory. God will deal us a good hand after a bad deal in life. He is a loving God that wants to see His children be successful.

He will fight for us. He will protect us. He will provide for us. He will grant us His grace and mercy. He will forgive us. He will restore us. When we understand what God will do for us; then we can put that bad hand in His hand!

No one will ever beat Him. You must believe that and know He has it all under control! The power of God's hand will knock the devil down for a knockout every time. The power of God's hand brings miracles in our lives. The power of God's hand sustains us until the promises of God come to pass. What a hand and I want that in my life!

Psalm 62:11-12

11 God hath spoken once; twice have I heard this; that power belongeth unto God.12 Also unto thee, O Lord, belongeth mercy: for thou renderest to every man according to his work.

We must learn to let God have his way in our lives. We will see Him do great things if we do this. God's hand is different from any man or woman. God's hand will provide an exit when you need it. He will make a way of escape for us. The bad hand you received can have you feeling frustrated. However, God knows how to deliver you; so, let me share an example from the Bible.

2 Kings 13:7, 14-19

7 Neither did he leave of the people to Jehoahaz but fifty horsemen, and ten chariots, and ten thousand footmen; for the king of Syria had destroyed them and had made them like the dust by threshing.

14 Now Elisha was fallen sick of his sickness whereof he died. And Joash the king of Israel came down unto him, and wept over

his face, and said, O my father, my father, the chariot of Israel, and the horsemen thereof.15 And Elisha said unto him, Take bow and arrows. And he took unto him bow and arrows.16 And he said to the king of Israel; Put thine hand upon the bow. And he put his hand upon it: and Elisha put his hands upon the king's hands.17 And he said, Open the WINDOW eastward. And he opened it. Then Elisha said, Shoot. And he shot. And he said, the arrow of the LORD's deliverance, and the arrow of deliverance from Syria: for thou shalt smite the Syrians in Aphek, till thou have consumed them.18 And he said, Take the arrows. And he took them. And he said unto the king of Israel, Smite upon the ground. And he smote thrice and stayed.19 and the man of God was wroth with him, and said, Thou shouldest have smitten five or six times; then hadst thou smitten Syria till thou hadst consumed it: whereas now thou shalt smite Syria but thrice.

Here in the text, there is king by the name Joash. He appears to have received a bad hand and had some issues. The new king the Bible states in verse two, "and he did that which was evil in the sight of the LORD, and followed the sins of Jeroboam the son of Nebat, which made Israel to sin; he departed not there from". The Lord's anger was kindled against Israel during this time.

God allowed the Israelites to be oppressed by Syria because of the idolatry. However, God loved them and had made a promise to Abraham. He promised to preserve a remnant. God didn't allow them to be wiped out. Sometimes we have a bad hand in life, because of being disobedient to God.

The war with the Syrians had affected them in a bad way. Their resources were very low as we observe in the seventh verse

"Neither did he leave of the people to Jehoahaz, but fifty horsemen, and ten chariots, and ten thousand footmen; for the king of Syria had destroyed them, and had made them like the dust by threshing."

Have you ever felt like you were in a battle and you lost stuff? The battle depleted your resources or your money. You used to be so happy, but now you're so uptight because of the bad hand. The bad hand has you stressed out. I want to encourage you that God's hand of deliverance will show up in your life, as you surrender to His will.

Here in the text, Josiah, the king begins to cry out. He goes to the prophet Elisha, who had been serving for about sixty years as a prophet. God began to forgive the king and Israel; even though they had rebelled against him. The king knew that Elisha was a great man of God. He addresses him as a father. However, he went crying and talked about their conditions.

He speaks of their depleted resources. He didn't understand that the Lord was the source of the resources. He didn't understand that God could send help from heaven with His mighty hand. He didn't understand that God could make a way out of no way. He didn't understand how God could give him victory; despite everything looking depleted.

I want to make an important point. We already have the victory. I want to encourage someone that God has already given you the victory through Jesus Christ. Christ was crucified for our sins. They took him down from the cross and put him in a grave. However, on the third day, he got up with all power and gave us victory and redemption.

We have victory over every disease and challenge. We receive healing because of the stripes of Jesus. Christ became poor that we might become rich. We are rich in his grace. We are rich in his mercy and favor. You're rich if Christ is your Savior!

Elisha, the prophet knew victory was coming, and he told Joash to take a bow and some arrows. Elisha said, "Draw the bow." The prophet was saying, "get ready to shoot." Are we ready for what God is about to do in our lives? Are you ready? Are you ready for your blessing? Are you ready for your healing? Are you ready for your breakthrough? Are you ready for your good hand from God's hand?

Elisha put his hand on the king's hand before he shot. Elisha let the king know this deliverance wasn't coming from his hand but God's hand. Elisha then said, "Shoot." The king shot. God has a way of reminding us that our blessings come from His hand and not ours. Our hands are limited as was Joash. Our talents, gifts, and resources are limited, but God isn't. We must understand that God can work through us. God can train us for victory if we're humble. He can train us to reign as David did.

Psalm 144:1-2

1. Blessed be the LORD my strength which teaches my hands to war, and my fingers to fight:

2 My goodness, and my fortress; my high tower, and my deliverer; my shield, and he in whom I trust; who subdueth my people under me."

God will give us good hands or make things better in our life. I propose a question, though? How bad do you want it? Will you take advantage of the opportunities God opens for you as your led by the Spirit? Joash would receive a challenge in this text.

He was tested, and he failed. Elisha would test the king. There is a test before the victory. He told him to take the arrows, and he took them. The prophet said, "Strike the ground." He struck three times and stopped. The prophet was angry with him and said, "You should have struck five or six times, and you would have destroyed Syria. However, now, you will only win three times. Joash was supposed to keep shooting or striking the ground, but he stopped.

He appeared to have no enthusiasm in the situation. God had told him through the prophet that deliverance was coming. We should have been excited! When God has declared, he is going to do something in our lives. We should have joy, excitement, and expectation. I don't know about you, but I get excited when God is moving in my life!

Joash may have been inexperienced in shooting the bow and arrows. However, God was not looking for skill or experience, but obedience and expectation. When we have obedience and expectation for God; it makes our spiritual ground ready for victory. Sometimes we must quit thinking we can do it with our hands or ability, but trust God's hand. I have learned expectation in God can produce enthusiasm. God wants to give us complete victory in our lives.

Joash shot or struck the ground three times and stopped. Three was not enough. The prophet said, "you should have kept going and reached five or six." The number five symbolizes God's grace and goodness toward humanity. God has plenty of grace for us if we keep going with expectation. God's hand is not slack, and he will bring us out. You must remember numbers twenty-three and nineteen!

Chapter 8 Caught up in the game

There are fifty-two cards in a deck. The fifty-two cards symbolize fifty-two weeks in a year. However, the spade is the suit that can cut other cards on the table; if the opportunity presents itself. The spade symbolizes old age and the final major season in our life if we're allowed to see it. It also has other meanings, such as the winter season, wisdom, and transformation. The hope is that we live to old age if we don't get caught up in the game.

God can do anything but fail. He can transform our lives and give us His wisdom. I want to encourage someone if God did it for us; He will do it for you! God has no respect of persons. It doesn't matter if it seems like you're caught up in the game. The Lord can bring you out and give you precious promises from his Word.

We see how people get caught up in the game in the inner city. Some end up dead or in jail. The devil desires that many get caught up in his web of deceit. The devil has webs that include selling drugs, guns, prostitution, and street life. The devil doesn't want you to make it to old age. He doesn't want you to walk in the wisdom of God.

Some may be thinking why many are so caught up in the game. Why are so many being shot every day? I understand how you feel; when it feels like you trapped in a game in the hood. I've been there too. It felt like I was dying slowly back then. I was caught up in the game. I have compassion for you because I'm from the hood.

I know what it is to sell drugs because I did it. I know what it is to lose my homeboys to the game. My vision was distorted back then because I was caught up. God opened my eyes and took the spiritual scales off, so I could see Him in 1997. He was there the whole time, but I had to surrender to Him. Man, that life was horrible; and was killing me. I share my testimony to show that God can bring transformation. God can bring change if we get rid of stuff that's killing us. We can start cutting stuff out like a spade when it presents itself.

I recall driving in my first car, a Nissan Sentra in the early nineties. I picked up a couple of my homeboys. We arrive at a church feeling sad because one of our homeboys was shot and killed. We had just seen him a couple of days before he was gunned down. I thought to myself it was foul how he got shot. He was making paper, but his fake friends were jealous. The fake friends even knew where my homey hid his stash and dope. They switched up on him and went where he had his stash.

They took his stash, and my homey found out about it. He confronted his fake friends, and it cost him his life. One of the traitors had a gun, and my homeboy didn't know, or he didn't think he would pull it. My homeboy turned his back after confronting them. The betrayer shot my homeboy in his dome, sending him to the hospital, then to the funeral home.

I was young sitting in the church with my homeboys crying. We played recreational football together, but a different game got him. We lost one of our soldiers. He was living the life, and the game wasn't kind to him. He got in the game selling cocaine, and he was making his loot. He probably was shocked to find out that his homies were out to get him. It's crazy like that in the hood. I wondered did he make it to heaven, so many people cried that day, including his family and friends. It was a hard pill to swallow.

The funeral made me think about life as the pastor preached the eulogy. I thought to myself, God; please let him make it to heaven because he was a good young man. He just got caught up in the game. He was trying to make some money to take care of his daughter and do some things for himself. He couldn't get a decent job due to his record. I'm looking back on it now. I wished he could have made better choices, but he was young, and his father wasn't in his life. He was misguided and misunderstood, like so many young black males. The preacher at the funeral brought up a scripture, which I remember to this day. The scripture was Romans 6:23.

Romans 6:23

For the wages of sin is death; but the gift of God is eternal life through Jesus Christ our Lord

I believe God was using the preacher that day. It was so many young black males at the funeral. I believe God was letting us know there are repercussions for how you live your life. A negative lifestyle can bring about self-destruction. The streets will catch back up with you. I knew it, and I think my home boys knew it too.

We just wanted that quick money and attention back then. God was in the hood. He was letting us know; this is not the life I ordained for you. I think we knew if we kept living the street life something was going to happen. We were making bad decisions, and our parents raised us better.

I'm looking back on it now, and we had warnings. God was in the hood, warning us to stop through our parents, grandparents, coaches, and other people. I realized that God loves us so much that He warns us to stop before destruction occurs. The devil is out to steal, kill, and destroy. We left the funeral that day sad for my homeboy and ready to blast. However, they had already arrested the cat that shot him.

We stopped at the store and got a lot of beer and white owls. We got to my apartment. We smoked so many blunts and poured out some beer for our homeboy. We would never see him again. God was in the hood like He always is. God is everywhere, and He knows all and sees everything. God was letting us know it's time to change, and I could feel it too.

I was caught up in the game. However, I am glad that God spared me and delivered me from the game! I am glad He delivered some of my friends from the game. My job is to warn others that God loves you and has a better life for you. You don't have to die in the game, because God has an abundant life for you with His promises.

God is a gentleman. God doesn't force Himself on anyone. We must receive him and his Word. God is not holding a gun to people's head and telling them to live the street life. People make choices; we must live with the choices we make in this life. I'm so glad that God is in the hood, waiting to show His love, grace, restoration, and mercy.

He desires us caught up with Him. He desires us hanging out with Him. God desires you free in Him, and not caught up in the devil's game of deception and lies. I believe God longs for us to live for Him. He is faithful, true, and He never lies. You can stand because God will not lie. It's in the Word, numbers twenty-three and nineteen!

Chapter 9 One night

I'm not a preacher who pretends to be so perfect and has no flaws. Those types of preachers don't exist if people would be real about it. God has brought me through a lot if I can share a little bit of it, and it helps someone else. I'm all for it, so let me share what happened to me one night.

God loves us so much that He will correct us and bring conviction in our lives. He corrects us because He wants to fulfill His promises in our life. He desires that we become who he has chosen us to be! He knows how to change our thinking. I know he changed my thinking one night. I experienced something over twenty-five years ago, and it changed me and my perspective. I learned that I was playing my cards the wrong way that night.

It brought conviction of how I was living. I remember chopping up some dope early in the morning. It was a Thursday, and I knew I was going to make some money that day. I was in a great mood because I had made some money the night before. Life was good in the hood. I chopped up some twenties, forties, and a piece for a hundred. I knew the area where I was going to chill for the day. I knew how much they normally would spend with me. I had it down to a science.

My homeboy scooped me up, and we headed to the spot. We got to the spot, and I was ready to get blazed up. I wanted to get my day started right with a blunt. Don't judge me; that's how it was for me back then. I was addicted to weed and beer.

I asked Big P man you got any blunts. He said, "No, I don't have any." I was like, "I got the weed, and you don't have the blunts." I said, "man, you're not worth a nickel." He said, "Take that to the store, homey." I was like, "what man you lame, and you broke." He said, "Whatever what about when I looked out for you." I was like, "man I am just messing with you homey, I got you." We laughed and walked out of the apartment towards the store, cutting through the path.

We walked through the path, and we ran into one of his neighbors from the complex. He was like, "what's up." I was like, "chilling man, that's about it." I didn't tell him we were going to get blunts. I knew he would have wanted to smoke. We talked for a few minutes, and then he said, "Slim, I'm going to talk at you later on." I said, "I'll be waiting on you." I thought to myself, yes money coming today. We get through the path and end up at the store. I bought the blunts and some brew, and we head back to the apartment. We got blazed up. I thought to myself it is going to be a long day, and it's not even noon yet.

We smoked blunts, drank beer, and watch TV that morning into the afternoon. I thought to myself this can't be the right. We're smoking, chilling, and most people are at work. I remember smoking and drinking so much I passed out sometime that afternoon. I woke up because my pager was vibrating, and I could feel it in my pocket on my thigh. I pulled it out and saw the number. The number twenty was behind it. I thought to myself it is on now.

After I started to wake up, I said, "What time is it, man"? My homeboy and a few other people were in the room now. I was like, "where did you guys come from"? They laughed and said, "you were sleeping on the couch when we got here." I was like, "wow"! My homeboy said, "it's almost seven o'clock." I had slept through most of the afternoon and some of the evening, that was some bomb weed.

I called the number back and told the guy to meet me at the spot near the path. I told my peeps I would be back. I must step out for a minute. My homeboy knew what that meant, but the others didn't. I stepped out of the apartment and headed towards the spot. We meet up, and it's a quick transaction. He gave me the cash I gave him the twenty. The dude said, "when are you going home, Slim." I said, "I will be here for a while, holler at me." He said, "Word will holler at you in a little bit." He had a couple of friends coming over. I went back to the apartment. I'm thinking it's going to be a long night, and I had better get myself together. I can't be out here sleeping and get caught off guard.

I got back to the apartment and got something to eat. I was hungry, and I hadn't eaten, and the weed gave me the munchies. We were chilling in the apartment, and my pager started vibrating again about an hour later. It's the same guy again. My homeboy was like, "you're blowing up man, let's get another sack (weed)." I said, "Nah homey, we can get another sack if you pay for it. I'll be right back, and I went out to the path. It's heating up this time it's for a forty.

I meet up with the guy and I could smell that he had been drinking. He was geeked up! I knew after this; he would be looking for more for him and his friends. He gives me the cash, and I give him the forty. Dude said, "yo they liking this man don't be surprised if we hit you up again." I said, "ok, I will be here." I'm thinking man I might have to stay the night and make this money.

I went back to the apartment with a smile on my face. My homeboy knew I was starting to make some money. He said, "yo he probably going to hit you up a couple more times they geeked up." I said, "I know, man I got to get this money." Big P replied, "my girl had to take the car to go to work." I was thinking ok he's not going to let me spend the night. I said, "I will catch a cab home."

Later, that night the same guy hit me up again: this time he got a sixty. Some more people around the hood had copped that nigh as well. It was a good night in the hood for me. However, I sense the night wasn't over, and I was right. It's a little after midnight, and I was about to call my cab to go to the crib. My pager started vibrating again. Yes, I thought this how you end the night. I look at my pager it is his number again, but this time it's for a hundred. I thought this was a good way to end my night, but I was wrong.

We meet at the spot, but this time he didn't have the cash. He said, "Follow me to my crib," I said what's up homey you trying to set me up." He said, "Nah man I'm waiting for my wife to give me my money she went to the store." I said, "Ok, and I followed him." I'm following with one of my hands in the right pocket of my jacket. My little three eighty was in my pocket. I had my three eighty for when things got shady. I didn't think he would give me a problem, but you never know in the hood.

We get to his apartment, and I go in with him. He said, "Hold on." He walked down the hall to get the money from his wife. I hear them arguing about the money, and how he was spending their rent and food money. I thought what's up with this guy. He told me he had friends over. Don't look like it to me. The apartment looked clean, and I don't even smell cigarette smoke. I thought something wasn't adding up. I stood there, thinking I need to leave this apartment. He was smoking up all this dope and taking from his household.

I was contemplating whether to leave or not as they argued, and a little girl came out of the room and looked at me. I could see the tears in her eyes. It shook me up, and her parents were back in their room, arguing over the money. I said to the little girl, "Are you ok." She shook her head and said, "No, I'm hungry." She came and hugged me on my leg as I stood there. I stooped down and hugged her. She recognized me from being in the neighborhood.

I felt so bad because I saw her before too, playing at the park with her little friends. I knew I was wrong. I thought to myself I could be the reason this child is not eating. I couldn't live with the thought of that. I reached in my pocket and gave her a piece of money, and I said that's yours and don't let anyone take it from you ok. She said, "ok." She was so happy about the money. The guy and his wife come out of the room, and they saw me talking to their daughter.

The wife was angry, and she said, "I'm not giving him no more money we don't have much left, and he is a crack head." I could see tears in her eyes. She sat down on the couch and said, "and he needs help." I said, "Man, you lied to me." He was smoking it up by his self. I didn't even try to make the transaction after that. I told the guy I wasn't coming by anymore.

The wife had tears in her eyes. I knew she loved the guy and her family. I didn't even know he was married and had a family. I left with so much conviction that night. I got back to the apartment and called a cab to go home. I thought to myself while riding in the cab. I started to see things from a different angle. I was messing up people live and families. I was messing up my life too. I knew it was time for a change. I knew I couldn't keep living life like that. I cared about people deep down in my heart. God was trying to tell me to stop what you're doing in the hood. It's destroying lives.

I was riding in the cab, feeling all this conviction. I didn't understand at the time God was dealing with me. God was in the hood, and in my situation, now that I look back on it. It was a crazy day and night as the cab pulled up at my crib. I paid the cab driver and went inside. It was one night I would never forget.

God forgave me, and He still brought His promises to pass in my life as I look back on that night! It was a night where I felt so guilty, and I knew it was time to stop selling. The Lord was letting me know it's time to get out of the game and do the right thing. God is good; I don't care what anyone has to say. God brought me from a very long way, and He is a promise keeper!

Chapter 10 Enough is enough

It took me a long time to figure out what the kings symbolized on the cards. They have meaning. The kings on the cards represent real kings such as King Alexander the Great (clubs), King Charlemagne (hearts), King Augustus Caesar (diamonds), and King David of Israel (spades). A king represents royalty. I used to feel good when I had a king of any suit in my hand. I felt like I can get at least a book with a king. All those years, I played spades and didn't realize that those cards symbolize something.

The king of spades represents King David of Israel. We all know how powerful and anointed David was. Well, guess what you're anointed to if you receive Christ. It's time for you to say enough is enough to your past.

The king of hearts represented King Charlemagne of France. He was another king that had ties to Christianity. I thought it was interesting to see that David is on a card. There may be some Christians who disagree with card playing, and I get that.

However, sometimes we're playing the game call life, but we don't recognize that we are kings too. We're royalty too, and we belong to the King of Kings, Jesus. I didn't recognize all those years those kings on the cards represented someone. We don't recognize what we have within us, or in our hands. It's time to wake up and be who God called us to be, and not who society thinks we should be. God wants to use us in his royal family. We are joint heirs of Christ if the Lord is our savior! (Romans 8:17)

I grew up in the hood and the struggle, but there came a time in my life, where I said enough is enough. There must be something better than this. Our God is the King of Kings, so we should walk like we're king's children. It must be something better than running the streets and being in the game. It must be something better than just barely making it. I was ready to thrive, not just survive. It must come to a point in your life where you say enough is enough.

Sometimes we deal with problems too long, but we don't have to. There is a loving God that has grace, mercy, healing, love, wisdom, peace, and joy. He also changes us from the inside out and makes us better people with character. We don't have to keep dealing with stuff that is stressing us out and destroying us. We can go to King Jesus for help. He is our answer. It's time to say enough is enough. We can be kings and queens. We're royalty made in the image of God!

Sometimes it can seem like you're going in a circle. You keep making the same mistakes, and God wants to end that cycle. He wants you to surrender to His will. He wants to give you another chance. You've e been dealing with this long enough. It's time to let God redirect you, so let's look at an example from the Word of God.

Deuteronomy 2:1-3

1 Then we turned, and took our journey into the wilderness by the way of the Red Sea, as the Lord spake unto me: and we compassed mount Seir many days.2 And the Lord spake unto me, saying,3 Ye have compassed this mountain long enough: turn you

northward.4 And command thou the people, saying, Ye are to pass through the coast of your brethren the children of Esau, which dwell in Seir; and they shall be afraid of you: take ye good heed unto yourselves therefore:5 Meddle not with them; for I will not give you of their land, no, not so much as a foot breadth; because I have given mount Seir unto Esau for a possession.6 Ye shall buy meat of them for money, that ye may eat; and ye shall also buy water of them for money, that ye may drink.7 For the Lord thy God hath blessed thee in all the works of thy hand: he knoweth thy walking through this great wilderness: these forty years the Lord thy God hath been with thee; thou hast lacked nothing.8 And when we passed by from our brethren the children of Esau, which dwelt in Seir, through the way of the plain from Elath, and from Eziongaber, we turned and passed by the way of the wilderness of Moab.

Here in this text, there is a transition going on with God's people. God tells Moses you have been at this mountain long enough. You have been facing this problem long enough. They had been in the wilderness for 40 years, going around in a circle. God said enough is enough. The people that doubted God and did not believe in Him died out. God reveals to Moses it's time a new generation to go in possess the land that He promised. God was giving a second chance to another generation. Moses was also dealing with transition because he was older. God had already told him that he was not going into the promised land. Joshua would be the leader, who would take the new generation into the promised land.

You may be thinking; how does this text apply to me? Well, maybe God is telling you that it's time to go in and possess what

God has for you. Maybe God is saying enough is enough. He is tired of seeing you suffer and wants to give you a better life. The Lord has better for you if you put Him first and have a relationship with Him.

God began to deal with them about their transition into the promised land in this text. He even provided instructions as they made the transition. God told them how to handle the other people; they would be meeting on their journey into the promised land. We must follow the instructions God gives us as we transition to a better life in Him.

Deuteronomy 2:4-8

4. And command thou the people, saying, Ye are to pass through the coast of your brethren the children of Esau, which dwell in Seir; and they shall be afraid of you: take ye good heed unto yourselves therefore:5 Meddle not with them; for I will not give you of their land, no, not so much as a foot breadth; because I have given mount Seir unto Esau for a possession.6 Ye shall buy meat of them for money, that ye may eat; and ye shall also buy water of them for money, that ye may drink.7 For the Lord thy God hath blessed thee in all the works of thy hand: he knoweth thy walking through this great wilderness: these forty years the Lord thy God hath been with thee; thou hast lacked nothing.8 And when we passed by from our brethren the children of Esau, which dwelt in Seir, through the way of the plain from Elath, and from Eziongaber, we turned and passed by the way of the wilderness of Moab.

When we make up our minds that enough is enough; it doesn't mean everything will be easy. However, it will be worth it. I this text God allows them to encounter people who already had their stuff. During this time, the Israelites didn't have their inheritance yet, because they were in their process. We cannot get jealous of others, who may have what we want as we're going through our process. It's on the way!

God told the Israelites don't mess with them or meddle with them. They were to stay focus on what God had for them. He wanted them to follow His instruction. God was about to give something better than what the other people had. He had taken care of them in the wilderness, and they lacked nothing. God is on your side even when you have a wilderness experience; you will lack nothing.

God wants you to rise and possess some things in your life. God desires to give you exposure to a better life. The best is yet to come. Don't settle for less when God has more for you; tell yourself enough is enough. It's time to rise from the pain.

It's time to rise from the disappointment. It's time to rise from the betrayal and forgive. It's time to rise and walk in your God-given purpose. It's time for the God-ordained man or woman to come forth. It's not over to God, say it's over; enough is enough. We must rise and quit crying. We must rise and embrace what God wants to do in our lives!

Let's be the generation that obeys God and possesses the land. Let's be the generation that listens to God and makes an impact on our families and the community. Are we ready to rise? Are we ready to let some stuff die? Are we ready for the transition? Are we ready for our second chance? Are we ready to say enough is enough? Are we ready to say I'm not who people say I am, but who God declares I am?

Enough is enough, and it's time to make changes. Enough is enough, and it's time to look at things from God's perspective rather than a man's perspective. What did God say about you in His Word? Our minds must embrace newness God's Word. God's perspective is his Word, and it always works! We can turn things around in our families and communities if we embrace the Word of God. We can possess what He has for us in the land.

Romans 12:1-2

1. I beseech you therefore, brethren, by the mercies of God, that ye present your bodies a living sacrifice, holy, acceptable unto God, which is your reasonable service.

2 And be not conformed to this world: but be ye transformed by the renewing of your mind, that ye may prove what is that good, and acceptable, and perfect, will of God.

God has called and chosen us, but we must present our bodies, our emotions, our very being to Him. We must live holy and have our minds renewed by the Word of God. It doesn't mean we will be perfect, but we must have renewed minds. We can then live a life that is pleasing to God. We can walk with maturity and faith. We will have a desire to do what is right, according to God's Word.

A truly renewed person will know what God is calling them to do. God will reveal His will for your life as your mind receives renewal. We all must let unbelief die in our mind. Enough is enough; do you want what God wants for your life? The Lord has an abundant life for us, and he promised it to us. He has an abundance of peace, joy, wisdom, understanding, blessings, and most of all, his presence in our lives. My brothers, my sisters, stand on the Word of God because He cannot lie. It's Numbers twenty-three and nineteen!

Chapter 11 A way of escape

I've had time to reflect since the Lord save me back in 1997. I have come to realize that there is a lot of oppression, poverty, economic disparity in the hood. Blacks are set up to fail in this country if you fall in the trap. However, God does make a way of escape. The way is through Jesus. You can do great things for God; it doesn't matter where you live. You can do great things if God has chosen you and empowered by his Spirit.

The hood or a bad situation is not your destination. It may be where you start in the fulfillment of your God-given destiny. However, it's not the end, and you can't blame everything on the white man. The precious promises of God are there for you too!

The Bible reveals that God used people from unlikely circumstances. They went on to do great things for him, their families, and their community. Don't let things like your past stop you; God has made a way of escape through Jesus Christ. God has more for you than you could ever imagine.

You may be saying I don't know if I can do great things. Truth is you can through Christ. Sometimes because you have been in a certain situation or place for a long time, it is hard to see yourself beyond that. God wants you to thrive, not just survive. There is nothing wrong with living in the hood if that is your choice. However, if God desires to do even more for you, why would you tell Him no? Why would you not believe?

There is an example in the Bible, where God brought the children of Israel out of slavery and bondage. However, the children of Israel had to realize how much God loved them. He wanted to see them blessed beyond anything they could have imagined. The Lord promised to bless them, but they had to trust God and take Him at His Word. God raised Moses, who was an Israelite by birth, to be a deliverer for Israel. God would bring them out through Moses.

However, the Bible lets us know that God made a way of escape, but the Israelites would have to change their mindset. The mindset of the people was important if they were going to walk in freedom. They got too comfortable being slaves, and it had messed up their perception of who God was. They thought all they could eat was, onions, cucumbers, fish, leeks, and garlic. God brings them out and declares I have a land flowing with milk and honey, which was far better than what they had. God wanted them to see themselves as landowners, business owners, and not slaves!

Numbers 11:5

5. We remember the fish, which we did eat in Egypt freely; the cucumbers, and the melons, and the leeks, and the onions, and the garlick.

God is everywhere. He is in the hood or any environment. He is ready to bless you with a life of peace and no lack. You may have the odds stacked against you, but God can turn it around. It may not be easy, but it is going to be worth it. God is taking you to the other side.

The enemy has set traps for you to fail because he knows God has a plan. God has a plan that is better than your plan. The life that God has for you is better than selling drugs. It's better than spending all your time getting high and living the street life. God has a plan that is better than being a prostitute.

The Devil is telling you that nothing is going to change if you live for God. I promise you if you stay committed to Christ, watch him bless you in the process. Watch God turn things around for you and make a way of escape. You will escape the street life if you surrender to Him. You will escape every addiction if you surrender to Him. He will help you! You will become a soldier for Christ if you do it His way. You will minister to people in jail instead of going to jail.

You may say, how can this be? The answer is God has made a way of escape through Christ. My brother, my sister God is everywhere, and He is in the hood too. I want you to remember that something good is coming out of this. When you give your life to Christ remember, promises are waiting on you. He has promised to be there for you. He has promised to provide for you. We must hold onto numbers twenty-three and nineteen! God has made a way of escape through Jesus Christ, but do you know who you are?

I spent a lot of years as a young person, not knowing who I was in God. I knew people who tried to tell me who I was, but I found out they were wrong. They were telling me out of their perspective. I decided to ask God, who I was in him. God began to reveal to me that I was not what people said about me. I was more than a drug dealer, hustler, or someone living the street life. I had low self-esteem because I had been through so much in the hood coming up.

God started showing me in His Word that I was someone in Him. He started revealing to me that He had plans for me, and it was not selling drugs. God started showing me that I was a blessed young man, but I had to know it. I began to realize who I was in Him and what His Word said about me. It changed my life forever. I would no longer be a victim from the hood, but an overcomer from the hood!

Whoever is reading this book do you know who you are? What did God say about you? What did He say about your purpose? I encourage you to develop your relationship with God through prayer and studying the Word. I encourage you to find a church and be a part of it. There is strength in numbers and surround yourself with God-fearing people. People who will love, encourage, and inspire you to push for more.

I want to encourage you that God loves you and has plans for you. The plans he has for you does not include the back seat of a police car. The plans he has for you doesn't have you incarcerated but liberated. The plan He has for you is being whole, and not a fragmented or torn to pieces. The Lord cares about you with an everlasting love. God desires that we be whole.

Jeremiah 29:11

11 For I know the thoughts that I think toward you, saith the Lord, thoughts of peace, and not of evil, to give you an expected end.

Do you know that God has plans for you? Do you know God is thinking about you? Do you know God has the best in store for you, but do you know who you are? Don't let the struggle, growing up in the hood, or a tuff environment make you second guess God. Don't let the devil trick you, because God has no respect of persons. He will bless you if you start walking with Him and trusting the process.

There was a young man in the Bible, who struggled with who he was. He didn't know who he was until God began to deal with him, and his name was Gideon. God saw Gideon as a mighty man of valor before Gideon even saw it. God knows more about us than we do because He made us. Gideon, at one point, saw himself as a poor insignificant person in his family, but God didn't see him that way.

God saw a strong man that would lead His people to victory over their enemies. God knew who he was. God knows who we are and what we will do. Gideon was encouraged by God despite his humble beginnings. We can't despise humble beginnings because the Lord can still raise us up.

Judges 6:11-16

11. And there came an angel of the Lord, and sat under an oak which was in Ophrah, that pertained unto Joash the Abiezrite: and his son Gideon threshed wheat by the winepress, to hide it from the Midianites.12 And the angel of the Lord appeared unto him, and said unto him, The Lord is with thee, thou mighty man of valour.13 And Gideon said unto him, Oh my Lord, if the Lord be with us, why then is all this befallen us? And where be all his miracles which our fathers told us of, saying, did not the Lord bring us up from Egypt? but now the Lord hath forsaken us, and delivered us into the hands of the Midianites.14 And the Lord looked upon him, and said, Go in this thy might, and thou shalt save Israel from the hand of the Midianites: have not I sent thee?15 And

he said unto him, Oh my Lord, wherewith shall I save Israel? behold, my family is poor in Manasseh, and I am the least in my father's house.16 And the Lord said unto him, Surely I will be with thee, and thou shalt smite the Midianites as one man.

God chooses this man, but he is still struggling with whether he can complete the mission. He seems to have some insecurity because of being poor. However, God still believes in him. I want to encourage you the Lord will empower you to complete his mission. God picks people from unlikely situations to be raised by Him, so He is glorified in their life.

Let's look at how God still used Gideon even though he had some concerns because of his background. Gideon was so fearful and unbelieving he asked God for a sign. Our God, out of love, permitted and answered Gideon's request.

Judges 6:17-23.

17 And he said unto him, If now I have found grace in thy sight, then shew me a sign that thou talkest with me.18 Depart not hence, I pray thee, until I come unto thee, and bring forth my present, and set it before thee. And he said, I will tarry until thou come again.19 And Gideon went in, and made ready a kid, and unleavened cakes of an ephah of flour: the flesh he put in a basket, and he put the broth in a pot, and brought it out unto him under the oak, and presented it.20 And the angel of God said unto him, Take the flesh and the unleavened cakes, and lay them upon this rock, and pour out the broth and he did so.21 Then the angel of the Lord put forth the end of the staff that was in his hand, and touched the flesh and the unleavened cakes; and there rose up fire

out of the rock, and consumed the flesh and the unleavened cakes. Then the angel of the Lord departed out of his sight.22 And when Gideon perceived that he was an angel of the Lord, Gideon said, Alas, O Lord God! for because I have seen an angel of the Lord face to face.23 And the Lord said unto him, Peace be unto thee; fear not: thou shalt not die.

We must all understand that when God calls us to a mission, He already knows the outcome. He desires that we trust Him, as He leads us on the mission. Are you ready for the mission? Are you ready to be who God called and chosen you to be? Or do you want to be who everybody else proclaims you to be? Do you know who you are? The Lord has a God-given purpose for your life that glorifies him. It's time to understand who you are in God and get on his mission for your life. The mission is going to be a way of escape!

Chapter 12 The mission

Life can be like a game of cards, and if that's the case, young lady, you're a queen. You're a queen like Rachel. She's the queen of diamonds. Young lady, you're a queen too, but stay on the mission God has for you. God has a man just for you, who won't mind working for you. Jacob worked a lot of years for Rachel. He truly loved her when they got married. God has a way of blessing His daughter that's mighty sweet. Young lady, you're someone special to God, please stay on the mission, and get ready for greatness!

Now let me encourage the brothers. I can't lie growing up in the hood had me on missions. Missions where I was trying to make some money any way I could; even it meant selling crack or weed. Missions if we had beef with cats. I wanted that quick money, easy money, but it was dangerous as well. You just never knew who would rob you. Who would snitch on you? Who was really on your side, because that's how it is in the hood?

I knew I had to be determined and willing to take a chance when on my missions back then. God showed me how to use those characteristics for Him. I started using my gifts and talents the right way. I have learned when God calls you from humble beginnings; He can use your bad and turn it around for good.

I started using my focus to study God's Word, got into prayer, and went to church regularly. I just felt so much better when God brought me back to Him many years ago. It was God that opened my eyes, and I will never take that credit. He opened my spiritual eyes, and I wanted to stay focus because of all the negativity. The more I focused on God, the more He revealed to me, who he was in my life.

A mind stayed on God; there is no telling how much that person can achieve. I want to encourage you to stay focus on God and be patient. It's not easy coming from the hood and then living a life completely for Christ. However, it is possible if you make up in your mind that you're not going back. Don't go back to a negative lifestyle, whether you continue to live in the hood or not. God has so much more; if you stay focus on the mission, that he puts you on.

Yes, I said, "the mission He puts you on." He will reveal to you what that mission is. God desires to do great things in our lives. The best place to be is in the center of His will for our lives. We must be committed to Christ when He is raising us to do His work. We must ask God what his will for our lives is; and He will give us understanding.

Ephesians 1:17-18

17 That the God of our Lord Jesus Christ, the Father of glory, may give unto you the spirit of wisdom and revelation in the knowledge of him:

18 The eyes of your understanding being enlightened; that ye may know what is the hope of his calling, and what the riches of the glory of his inheritance in the saints.

I'm so glad God doesn't leave us in the dark but lets us know who we are in Him. He has a divine plan for our lives, and we are not just here to live an unproductive life. God has a purpose for us. It doesn't matter what the mission it is; God sees us as valuable. The Enemy wouldn't be messing with you if you weren't valuable. However, we must know that we're valuable, and God has us on a mission.

I remember when I was out in the world, and when I wanted something, I was determined to get it. I had a determined attitude, and I felt like no one could stop me. I had to learn to keep that same attitude when I got saved but in a positive manner. Once I realized that God was with me, I became so determined to complete my mission. I was determined to live for Christ despite opposition, coming from the hood, and people misunderstanding me. I knew God had called me, so I had to answer to him at the end of the day.

Determination in Christ will take you a long way in fulfilling your God-given purpose. I refused to give up because of God's Word. I could do what He called me to do. God's Word let me know I could be a warrior for Christ through it all.

Philippians 4:13

13 I can do all things through Christ, which strengtheneth me.

God will strengthen us as we go about completing His missions. He will give us grace and mercy to accomplish His will for our lives. We are victorious in Christ. We will win my friends.

You can have assurance and determination on the mission because God sees you doing great things for Him. God said in his Word, "we are more than a conqueror." God declared that about us, so don't let anything stop you in your process. It will be some rough days but stay determined and keep pushing. You're a champion and look what God said about you!

Romans 8:37

37. Nay, in all these things we are more than conquerors through him that loved us.

Things will happen to make you want to give up but stay determined to finish the race. God said, "in all these things, we are more than conquerors." Paul was talking about the things that will come up on the mission, to separate us from God and His love. We must hold fast to God when the enemy is trying to tell us to throw in the tile. Don't let anyone or anything separate you from the love of Christ.

Romans 8:35-39

35 Who shall separate us from the love of Christ? shall tribulation, or distress, or persecution, or famine, or nakedness, or peril, or sword?36 As it is written, For thy sake we are killed all the day long; we are accounted as sheep for the slaughter.37 Nay, in all these things we are more than conquerors through him that loved us.38 For I am persuaded, that neither death, nor life, nor angels, nor principalities, nor powers, nor things present, nor things to come,39 Nor height, nor depth, nor any other creature, shall be able to separate us from the love of God, which is in Christ Jesus our Lord.

When I think about determination in Christ, I also think about taking a chance. There will be times when God will challenge us on the mission. A challenge to take a chance or step out on faith. We must trust God in the storms of life. We must realize in our process that there is a spiritual war going on with an enemy. He desires to stop our progress. My brothers, my sisters, keep pressing and stand on the promises of God.

Chapter 13 There's a war going on

There's a war going on in the hood. The war has our youth fighting, shooting, and killing each other. There is also a spiritual war going on in our families, communities, and churches. There is a spiritual war going on for our progress. However, we must learn that there is a better way and stop killing each other. God wants us to learn how to fight His way.

We must learn that God is real, and He wants to win the war for us. We must value him and let him be in our lives. The devil desires to destroy so many young black men because he sees your potential. The enemy knows you are physically and mentally strong. The enemy knows if you can survive in the hood. You can probably survive anywhere and do great things once you realize that.

Don't let the enemy deceive you into thinking, that's all life has to offer is selling drugs, gang banging and living the street life. God has so much to offer, and you don't have to live like that. God has so much for us if we can think outside of the box per se. God owns it all, and he can bless you.

Listen if you can bag up drugs, hide from cops, enemies, and still make money; you can become a real businessperson. Imagine what you could do if you did it the right way. I want you to imagine having a legal business, making even more money, and not having to worry about enemies and cops. You already have the right mindset to do business. You must change the way you do it. It is time for you to become a business owner instead of a drug dealer. A business owner can bring change in a positive way to the hood, rather than being a drug dealer. A drug dealer is hurting the inner city because of the lives lost to the game, and people become addicted to drugs.

The war is on in the streets without question, being orchestrated by the enemy behind the scenes. The devil is real, and he has waged war on the inner city. It's time that we rise and live for God, who created us to be soldiers in His army. The Lord is the only one that has already defeated the devil. Why wouldn't you want to be on his team? You don't have to keep losing battles in life because you don't have anyone. The Lord is someone that will stick with you through the thick and thin. God will stick with you, my brother, my sister. The Lord is strong in battle!

The Lord will fight for you in every situation if you surrender to His will. You cannot lose with God. No one can defeat God. It's a war going on for our soul, and the only one that will give us victory is God. When will you let Him fight for you? When will you let Him show you that He is a provider? When will you let Him show you that He will never leave you or forsake you? When will you let Him show you that He will give you peace instead of chaos?

It's time for God to give you victory in this war. It's time for you to start winning some battles the right way. The Lord wants you to win battles in your mind. He desires that you win battles with legal money. He wants you to win battles by showing you; how to be a real man loving yourself, your family, and the community. It's time to win in God and prove all those people wrong.

They believed you would never be anything. God will fight for a better you if you let Him. God will prove the doubters wrong!

It's a fixed fight, and God will reveal His glory in your life if you let Him. The Word of God gives us examples. How the fight was fixed, and all God's people had to do was trust Him. The Lord desires that we be obedient, so and He can bless us. Sometimes we make things harder than they are. Let's look at the Word of God for a minute.

Isaiah 40: 1-5

1. Comfort ye, comfort ye my people, saith your God.2 Speak ye comfortably to Jerusalem, and cry unto her, that her warfare is accomplished, that her iniquity is pardoned: for she hath received of the Lord's hand double for all her sins.3 The voice of him that crieth in the wilderness, Prepare ye the way of the Lord, make straight in the desert a highway for our God.4 Every valley shall be exalted, and every mountain and hill shall be made low: and the crooked shall be made straight, and the rough places plain:5 And the glory of the Lord shall be revealed, and all flesh shall see it together: for the mouth of the Lord hath spoken it.

Here in this text, the tone begins to change. Chapters one through thirty-nine the prophet speaks of warning God's people, that judgment was coming. Isaiah, the thirty-ninth chapter speaks of the Babylonians invasion and the people of God. The Israelites went into exile and captivity. However, in chapter forty of the book, Isaiah, the tone of the book begins to shift. The writer or prophet begins to speak about comfort, blessing, and the glory of the Lord coming.

The writer said comfort ye, comfort ye. God was saying through the prophet that I'm going to comfort you in your struggle. We serve a God that loves us, and He will comfort us no matter what we are going through. He is the God of all comfort.

2 Corinthians 1:3

3 Blessed be the God and Father of our Lord Jesus Christ, the Father of mercies and God of all comfort.

God was letting his people know that he was going to comfort them even though they had messed up. They were taken into captivity by the Babylonians. He was going to bring them out and back to Jerusalem to their place of blessing. Sometimes as children of God, it can seem like we are in captivity because of a spiritual war. It seems like you try to go forward and you get knocked back ten more steps. It seems like nothing is working. It seems like bad things are going on in your family and seems like life is stressing you out. It seems like you cannot break through.

Notice I said, "seems like," because you're experiencing a fixed fight and God has already declared you victorious through Christ Jesus. We're not trying to win; God has already declared us winners. Is there a process to go through? The answer is yes. However, Christ has already won the war for us. He won the war for us when He died on the cross of Calvary. They placed Him in a grave, but the third day He rose with all power!

God will comfort us, but we must hold on. We must hold on to God's hand because He will never leave us or forsake us. He always makes us winners and conquerors over situations in our lives.

Romans 8:37-39

37 Nay, in all these things we are more than conquerors through him that loved us.38 For I am persuaded, that neither death, nor life, nor angels, nor principalities, nor powers, nor things present, nor things to come,39 Nor height, nor depth, nor any other creature, shall be able to separate us from the love of God, which is in Christ Jesus our Lord.

Isaiah 40:2

2. Speak ye comfortably to Jerusalem, and cry unto her, that her warfare is accomplished, that her iniquity is pardoned: for she hath received of the Lord's hand double for all her sins.

The text brought up a point, which was "that her warfare has ended." There comes a time in our lives, when I believe God says enough is enough. I'm going to bless my people, and they have learned their lesson. Notice the text said, and their sins had been forgiven or pardoned.

How have our sins been pardoned? The finished work of Jesus Christ pardons our sins. Christ paid it all on the cross of Calvary. Christ died for us, so why are you letting people take you through a guilt trip? God has already forgiven you! Christ forgave you, so forgive yourself. We must get our minds ready to receive what God has for us. It is a spiritual war going on; we must get our minds right in God.

The children of Israel realized they had messed up and were suffering for it in this text. God saw their suffering and comforted them. He blessed them and revealed His glory. God has already declared that He is going to comfort us, bless us, and there is nothing the enemy can do about it! We must stay in His will for our lives, and he will do just what He said. God will reward us if we stay faithful and keep our faith in Him. We must stay faithful to God like we were faithful to the streets. You must stay faithful to God like you stayed faithful to hanging on the block, or in the clubs. God wants you to turn that mentality around by staying faithful to Him. He will reward you in the process.

Hebrews 11:6

6. But without faith it is impossible to please him: for he that cometh to God must believe that he is, and that he is a rewarder of them that diligently seek him.

Isaiah 40:3

3 The voice of him that crieth in the wilderness, Prepare ye the way of the Lord, make straight in the desert a highway for our God.

Our hearts are the road or the highway that God is using to reveal His glory in our lives. The idea of preparing the way of the Lord is like a word picture. The real preparation must take place in our hearts. Building a road takes a lot of construction. Our hearts and minds are under spiritual construction, and Christ is the engineer. Constructing or building a highway is very much like the preparation God must do in our hearts. We're under God's construction, a work in progress!

God believes in you, and since He believes in you; start preparing for a better life in the Lord. He works on our minds so that He can fulfill His plan and purpose for our lives. He is preparing us for the great things he has in store for us. God has a way of blessing us, after teaching us in the valley, and bring us up out of the valley. When there seems like a mountain or obstacle, God has a way of removing challenges, if our hearts are right towards him. Our minds must be committed and willing to trust God. God's glory will show up in our lives.

It's a war going on, but we already have the victory! God knows how to make the crooked straight. He knows how to turn things around that seem impossible and make them possible. We must surrender and let him prepare our hearts.

Isaiah 40:4-5

4 Every valley shall be exalted, and every mountain and hill shall be made low: and the crooked shall be made straight, and the rough places plain:5 And the glory of the Lord shall be revealed, and all flesh shall see it together: for the mouth of the Lord hath spoken it. I encourage you to keep fighting the good fight of faith as God gives you the victory! When we stay with the Lord, the victory is guaranteed. God will perform what He has spoken over our lives.

1 Timothy 6:12

12. Fight the good fight of faith, lay hold on eternal life, whereunto thou art also called, and hast professed a good profession before many witnesses.

Please remember it's a war going on for your soul. It's a war going on for your destiny. It's a war going on for your family and community. It's time to step up to the challenge in this war. Are you ready for the challenge?

Chapter 14 Poison

The Big Joker is the highest spade. It trumps all the cards in the deck. I want you to understand something. The devil is the big joker in life. He is a joke. However, he is powerful, and the only one that trumps him is God. I thought the big joker got me several years ago and let me explain.

I remember my grandmother telling me; God was going to use me. I didn't know to what extent before she died in 1995. I kept was she said about me all these years. I have watched the promises of God come to pass in my life. I know God is not through with me yet.

When I answered the call to ministry in 1997, I didn't know so much would come with it. I love helping and serving people; that's my passion. However, there is a flip side to it. It's called spiritual warfare. The devil is not happy when you serve and help other people. You become a target, especially if you're preaching the Gospel of Jesus Christ. When you preach Jesus, it makes the enemy mad!

However, down through the years, I felt God calling me into a deeper spiritual walk with Him. I began preaching in 1999. God told me that He would use me to teach and preach the Gospel. I saw God moving in my life even as a young preacher. After I would preach some people would say that was an on-time word. I needed to hear that, Hayes. I knew it was God using me and always said, "To God be the glory."

However, I noticed sometimes that others became jealous of how God was using me. I felt mistreated by some, while I preached in the Body of Christ. I've learned to be stronger not let that get me down because rejection happens when you're truly preaching the Gospel. I stayed focused but in 2008, I felt like throwing in the towel.

I remember during this time that I was going through a lot financially. I also remember studying some scriptures about how the Lord desires to use you in the Bible. The text was in Luke the nineteenth chapter verse twenty-eight through forty. I was excited, and I knew God was up to something in my life. I also had released my Gospel rap album "The Apocalypse."

The excitement came to a screeching halt the fall of 2008, so it seemed. One day I was invited to an event. I believe someone put some poison in my drink or food that day. I remember going home to my studio apartment at that time in pain. My stomach was hurting, and I began to throw up. It certainly didn't feel like God was using me. It felt like I was getting ready to die.

I stayed in my apartment for a couple of days, and it didn't get better. However, on the third, after being poisoned, I attempted to go to work. I began to drive my car down the street not too far from where I lived. I remember getting to a stop sign leading out of the neighborhood, and things started to get very blurry. I started to breathe hard.

I remember feeling scared and alone. I said to God, "Please don't let me die like this." It just felt like I was getting ready to leave out of here. I recall that it felt like I was going to pass out. I was able to get my car off the road and onto the shoulder. I remember sitting in my car with the flashers on, and people drove right past me. I felt so weak.

I remember that I started to pray, and I asked God to help me. I remember sitting there debating should I call 911 or not. I waited a few minutes to see if I could catch my breath and feel better. I slowly started feeling better. My vision started to come back to normal. It was nothing but the power of God that touched me at that moment in my life. I know for myself that God is a promise keeper. He has proclaimed in His word that I will never leave you or forsake you.

I sat in my tan Mitsubishi slumped over, with my head on the steering wheel, praying to the Lord. I asked God to help me get back to my apartment. I felt like I would be ok if I made it back home. God gave me the strength to make it back home. I opened the door, and I hurried to lie down on the couch. My head was spinning, and I thought to myself, I better get some help. It didn't feel like I was going to make it.

I called one of my friends, and they took me to the hospital. My friend was like what's going on, Tony. I remember telling them that someone at the event had put something in my food. My friend was angry and upset and was like, "who did this"? I said, "I don't know." I told my friend if something happened to me, please let someone know.

After receiving treatment for whatever was going on with me that day; I slept for a long time in the emergency room. The doctor came in after I woke up several hours later and said, "I see you're up now. I wondered how long I had been asleep. They told me for several hours. The medicine knocked me out. The funny part about it the doctor was like, "I'm not sure what's going on with you." He thought it was just a virus. I knew it was more than a virus.

He sent me home late that night, and I still didn't feel good. I got home and took some of the medicine they prescribe for me. I had an allergic reaction. I was throwing up and shaking like a crack head or something. I thought to myself what kind of medicine this is. Well, I ended back up in the hospital again. They gave me something for the allergic reaction. It felt like I was never going to get well.

I was sick for months, and the doctors couldn't tell me what was wrong with me. I went to the emergency room several times. They would say, "it's a virus." I just knew I had to beat this poison or whatever was in my body. It was a tuff fight for about three months. However, the fight took its toll on me; I became depressed. It felt like it was the end. It also felt like I was in a hole, and I couldn't get out.

I was depressed because I was self-employed at that time. I couldn't take care of myself because of the sickness due to the poison and now depression. I couldn't eat that much, and I was losing weight. I couldn't sleep at night, and I had panic attacks due to depression. When I tried to work, I felt so weak and would have to come home. I thought to myself, God, where are you? Lord, will I make it. God, do you love me? Why am I going through this Lord? I didn't do anything to anybody.

I lost all I had due to my sickness and depression. I had to stay with a friend. I felt so embarrassed and weak. My life had changed quickly. I remember before I went to bed one night, I cried to the Lord. He heard my cry. I recall asking God to help me and heal me from the poison and the depression. I couldn't take it anymore. I sat down on the bed, and I opened the Bible to Isaiah, chapter fifty-three, and verse five. God told me to speak that scripture for twenty-one days. I got up every day after that and began to speak the word of God.

At first, it seemed like I got worse, however a week or so later I began to feel better. I started to eat more, and that was a challenge all by itself. Some days I had to force myself to eat because I didn't have an appetite. God was starting to heal me, and I sensed it. My strength was slowly but surely coming back. However, I still couldn't sleep at night, and the panic attacks were still there.

A month or so later, I got up early one Sunday morning, and I felt the Holy Spirit. I sensed that God was going to do something that day. I prepared for church with praise on my lips. I remember praising God before we even made it to church that day. When the service started the power of God fell in the church that morning. I felt so much joy and peace.

We had a guest speaker that morning. He preached, and after his message, he had an altar call. The altar was filled with people that morning, and the glory of God was around that altar. I remember people getting delivered at the altar. I said to myself, "I'm tired of this sickness." I went down to the altar for prayer.

I got to the altar, and all the altar workers were busy praying for other souls. I was waiting, and the Holy Spirit told me to get on my knees and pray on the altar. I obeyed God. I got on my knees and asked God to heal me completely from that poison and depression. As I started to pray, I felt the Holy Spirit come over me, and I felt warm. I cried out to God!

As I cried on the altar, God told me it's done you're healed, son. When I got up, I felt brand new. I knew I had experienced God healing me. I remember I jumped and praised God, and I didn't care who saw me. All the pain, sickness, depression, and panic attacks were gone. I felt great again. Tears of joy streamed down my face! My God is a healer. My God is a promise keeper. He told me He was going to heal me, and He did. God can't lie and let me tell you why it's numbers twenty-three and nineteen!

Chapter 15 Step up to the challenge

It's not always easy to forgive or adjust, especially when bad things have happened to you. It takes time for wounds to heal. Sometimes we must learn to forgive ourselves. Sometimes we must forgive others in our healing process. Is it easy? The answer is no, to be honest. However, it's worth it because our souls need to be free again. Our souls still hunger and thirst for God, our creator.

Sometimes we must step up to the challenge. It's easy to throw the tile in, and give up, or not forgive. God lets us know through our souls, that there is more to live for in Him. You can forgive yourself, especially if you know you didn't do anything wrong. God has more for you, and this why you're still here. You have a purpose through all the pain.

We must free ourselves by forgiving those who have offended us. Bad things will happen while we live this life. However, we must step up to the challenge. We have to say to ourselves this is not how my story ends! God has a better ending than this. Sometimes we must go to counseling or get professional help; but whatever it takes step up to the challenge.

We must step up because; God can give us a better hand through His grace and mercy. God promised never to leave us or forsake us. The devil plots and schemes but God has a better plan. A better plan where you win, and you're no longer a victim but a victor. God can turn around our humble beginnings, misfortunes, abuse, hurt, and pain through His power. There is nothing too hard for God. It's time to tell that spiritual giant you're facing, that you're coming down in Jesus name!

The Bible lets us know that giants do fall! We don't have to spend our lives in fear of spiritual giants but defeat them. Do you believe that the giants in your life are coming down? Let's look at the Word of God for a minute.

1 Samuel 17: 37-53

37 David said moreover, The Lord that delivered me out of the paw of the lion, and out of the paw of the bear, he will deliver me out of the hand of this Philistine. And Saul said unto David, Go, and the Lord be with thee.38 And Saul armed David with his armour, and he put an helmet of brass upon his head; also he armed him with a coat of mail.39 And David girded his sword upon his armour, and he assayed to go; for he had not proved it. And David said unto Saul, I cannot go with these; for I have not proved them. And David put them off him.40 And he took his staff in his hand, and chose him five smooth stones out of the brook, and put them in a shepherd's bag which he had, even in a scrip; and his sling was in his hand: and he drew near to the Philistine.41 And the Philistine came on and drew near unto David; and the man that bare the shield went before him.42 And when the Philistine looked about, and saw David, he disdained him: for he was but a youth, and ruddy, and of a fair countenance.43 And the Philistine said unto David, Am I a dog, that thou comest to me with staves? And the Philistine cursed David by his gods.44

And the Philistine said to David, Come to me, and I will give thy flesh unto the fowls of the air, and to the beasts of the field.45 Then said David to the Philistine, Thou comest to me with a sword, and with a spear, and with a shield: but I come to thee in the name of the Lord of hosts, the God of the armies of Israel, whom thou hast defied.46 This day will the Lord deliver thee into mine hand; and I will smite thee, and take thine head from thee; and I will give the carcases of the host of the Philistines this day unto the fowls of the air, and to the wild beasts of the earth; that all the earth may know that there is a God in Israel.47 And all this assembly shall know that the Lord saveth not with sword and spear: for the battle is the Lord's, and he will give you into our hands.48 And it came to pass, when the Philistine arose, and came, and drew nigh to meet David, that David hastened, and ran toward the army to meet the Philistine.49 And David put his hand in his bag, and took thence a stone, and slang it, and smote the Philistine in his forehead, that the stone sunk into his forehead; and he fell upon his face to the earth.50 So David prevailed over the Philistine with a sling and with a stone, and smote the Philistine, and slew him; but there was no sword in the hand of David.51 Therefore David ran, and stood upon the Philistine, and took his sword, and drew it out of the sheath thereof, and slew him, and cut off his head therewith. And when the Philistines saw their champion was dead, they fled.52 And the men of Israel and of Judah arose, and shouted, and pursued the Philistines, until thou come to the valley, and to the gates of Ekron. And the wounded of the Philistines fell down by the way to Shaaraim, even unto Gath, and unto Ekron.53 And the children of Israel returned from chasing after the Philistines, and they spoiled their tents.

Here in this text, we have the main character, which is David. David is a young man on a mission, who is sent by God. He is on a mission that God has already prepared him for, but he must accept the challenge. He must accept the challenge and go!

David's father sends him to see about his brothers and the army of Israel. Goliath was the champion of the Philistines. He mocked God's people for forty days. He just knew no one could beat him, but that was not true. It wasn't that no one could beat him. He was just good at making the Israelites walk in fear. They were afraid and intimidated by him, because of his size. They were also afraid of him because of his words. These fear tactics had everybody in the army of Israel scared of him.

The giant showed up for forty days and would taunt the people of God. He would and say, "send me a man that will fight me." No one would step up to the plate and fight him, not even Saul. Saul was the tallest man for Israel, but he would not step up to fight him. Everybody would run away when Goliath showed up, and this went on for 40 days.

Spiritual giants keep showing up in your life to intimidate you. Spiritual giants that try to deceive you; and tell you that you can't make it, but the devil is a liar. A giant that tells you to doubt God, that giant is a liar. Giants that show up, and bring up your past, that giant is a liar. Your sins are forgiven if you have asked Christ into your life. Giants that tell you that no one loves you, that giant is a liar. God loves and cares for you, and He has people set up to love you.

Giants that try to keep you in poverty, that giant is lying to you. Giants that tell you, your situation will never change, the devil is a liar. God has plans for you, and He is freeing you up to do great things for Him. It's time to step up to the challenge and knock these giants down spiritually. We can do it through Jesus Christ, our Savior!

We have David as an example. He shows up at the camp and hears this giant talking. David was like "who is this uncircumcised Philistine." The giant was talking junk to them and call himself disrespecting God. David was ready to step up to the challenge, but he wanted to get more information concerning this challenge. Sometimes we need to get information on what we are about to defeat because there may be a reward or a blessing for us.

Big challenges or risks come with great rewards. God was setting David up for greatness. Whenever God is bringing a challenge in our life; we must understand there is a reward in it for us. One of the reasons why the enemy wants us to run from the challenge because there is a promotion attached to it. There is a breakthrough attached to it. There is a new life with success attached to it!

The enemy uses fear to make us run from the challenge when the challenge could be a blessing. It's time to show up and do what God has called us to do. It's time to show up and say, "what's in it for me." You have been through enough! It's time to show up and get rid of the fear.

God has a great reward for us if we accept the challenge. We must step up and take the challenge because of our purpose. It's going to lead us to our destiny in God. It's going to take the reproach off you. It's going to take the reproach off your family and ministry.

I Samuel 17:26

26 And David spake to the men that stood by him, saying, what shall be done to the man that killeth this Philistine, and taketh away the reproach from Israel?

Sometimes there is reproach that God wants us to take away from our lives. The Bible speaks about it in several passages. How God's people sometimes lived in a state of reproach. The reproach is a state of shame and disgrace. This type of reproach resulted in them becoming a laughingstock, they had to endure the ridicule, mocking, and scoffing of onlookers. Sometimes you must ask yourself is there a reproach in my life? It's time for that reproach to go, by stepping up to the challenge.

In this text, Israel had a reproach; what was the reproach? It was a shame, because Goliath had them shook and afraid. They had a reproach of fear on them. They had a reproach of disappointment on them, and it was making them look bad. God doesn't want us walking around in shame.

God doesn't want us walking in fear. God doesn't want us to walk in disappointment. Sometimes there is a reproach of barrenness. You have tried so long, and it seems like nothing is coming forth as you imagined. However, if you step up to the challenge, the reproach can be taken away by the power of God.

It's time to step up! How do we step up and take the challenge? We step up by realizing that this battle or situation is a spiritual one. We must see through the eyes of faith. We must see it from God's perspective and not a man's perspective. God desires to show His mighty power in our lives, but we must step up to the challenge. (Ephesians 1:17-19)

David began to sense that it was his time. I believe David had been waiting for his time to shine. He had the experience and the skills, to get the victory through God. He had a relationship with God. God let David know he could beat this huge giant. When we have a relationship with God, he will let us know what we can do through Him.

God had already delivered him from the bear and the lion, so he knew he could defeat this giant. Everything you have been through has prepared you for your defining moment. God gives us defining moments to defeat our giants. You can do it because God has prepared you. God has given you the green light. The green light from God is the indicator you're about to win!

Don't get upset when people don't believe in you. David's oldest brother and Saul didn't believe that he could do it. They were tall and should have been out there fighting. However, they were scared to fight for the Lord and His people. God will bless us if we step up because our families and communities will experience victory too, as we win.

David was making them look bad, and his brother got mad about him being there. The way God is going to use you; it's going to make some people look bad. Some people will be upset about it. My brothers, my sisters, stay humble and let God use you! David went from the sheep pasture to the palace. He would be trained to be a king. God will promote us if we step up to the challenge.

Psalm 76: 4-6

4. I said unto the fools, Deal not foolishly: and to the wicked, Lift not up the horn:5 Lift not up your horn on high: speak not with a stiff neck.6 For promotion cometh neither from the east, nor from the west, nor from the south.

Don't use someone else stuff but use what God has given you. God has equipped us so we can step up. We must use what God has already put in us. Be yourself whether people understand you or not! David couldn't walk in Saul's armor because it didn't fit him. He could have been killed trying to use something that didn't fit him. He used what he was comfortable with, which was the slingshot and stones.

We must use our faith and put on the armor of God because the battle is not ours but God's. David begins to speak victory. He told the giant what he was going to do to him before it even happened. We must learn to speak victory before we even see the results.

1 Samuel 17:45-47

45 Then said David to the Philistine, thou comest to me with a sword, and with a spear, and with a shield: but I come to thee in the name of the Lord of hosts, the God of the armies of Israel, whom thou hast defied.

46 This day will the Lord deliver thee into mine hand; and I will smite thee, and take thine head from thee; and I will give the carcases of the host of the Philistines this day unto the fowls of the air, and to the wild beasts of the earth; that all the earth may know that there is a God in Israel.

47 And all this assembly shall know that the Lord saveth not with sword and spear: for the battle is the Lord's, and he will give you into our hands.

Proverbs 18:21

21. Death and life are in the power of the tongue: and they that love it shall eat the fruit thereof.

After we get through speaking; it's time to go towards the problem. David said what he had to say, and the giant got mad. He started moving towards David. David didn't run away but ran towards the giant. He stayed calm and got close enough and then reached into his bag. He got a slingshot and a stone. He then shot his shot, and God got behind the rock or stone. The stone hit the giant in the head, and it sunk in. The power of God made the stone sink in the head of the giant; killing him at that very second. The power of God had given David, and the people the victory.

David cut his head off to make sure he was dead and brought back the evidence to Jerusalem. He let everybody know God gave me this victory. He had the evidence so that he could get his reward. David's life changed forever on that day. He became a hero of the faith!

When God gets through with us, we will have the evidence of the victory. People will know that the Lord is on our side. People will see that we stepped up to the challenge, and the power of God showed up on our behalf. My brother, my sister, it's time to step up because God has a great hand for you. We have to step up, show up, and receive it because God doesn't lie.

Numbers 23:19

Chapter 16 Spiritually ashy

We must stay focus if we are going to receive the precious promises of God in our life. We cannot allow our relationship with God to become dry. Our relationship with God should be alive and well, and not dried up like a prune. God doesn't want to fellowship with us like that.

There is nothing like taking a warm shower or bath. Most of us put lotion on to get rid of the ash after a shower. It's not a good look to be walking around looking dry and ashy, because you haven't put on lotion. Sometimes spiritually, we are walking around ashy or dry. God doesn't want us to be ashy but moisturized with a desire of praise for Him.

Sometimes we have become dry because of situations. Dryness has set in because of the struggle. Dryness has set in because of the storms of life. It's time to say, "enough with the dryness and being spiritually ashy." I remember one time I was at work, and I was so ashy. A lady came and gave me some lotion. I had taken a shower but didn't put on any lotion. She was like, "take this lotion I'm tired of looking at your ashy self today"

God can see that we are spiritually ashy, but so can others. People can see your nasty attitude and the bad way you treat other people. People can see that you're bitter. People can see that you're not praising and worshipping God. God and people can see our dryness. God, however, doesn't hold it against you but desires for us to repent and thirst for Him.

Life can make us dry and spiritually ashy. God desires to quench our thirst. Our soul is yearning for more of God. I like drinking sodas! I know sodas aren't good for us. However, I have learned that sodas, coffee, tea, and other beverages don't quench our thirst. The body is yearning for more water. Water alone quenches the thirst of the body. It's water that provides nutrients to the body, removes waste, regulates the temperature of the body, and renews the body. Those other beverages can't do what water does. Water alone does great things to the body.

Our soul is yearning for God alone. When God made us, He left a spiritual part of us; that can only be filled and moisturize by Him. I have noticed that my skin dries out faster in some environments because of the dryness. Sometimes the environments that we have grown up in have caused spiritual dryness. It has caused us to be spiritually dry and ashy because God was not welcome in that environment. The presence of God was not flowing in that environment.

God is our water and sustainer of life, and if God is not present in our life, we will become dry. The dryness can lead to droughts in our lives. Those droughts can affect our very being and our spiritual life. It can affect our minds, bodies, families, resources, and money. We must stay hydrated and moisturize in God, per se!

God longs to clean us up with a spiritual bath. He desires to wash us with His Word. We must learn to put some spiritual lotion on after the washing. I've learned this is an ongoing process. You might be saying what spiritual lotion is that? I'm talking about thirsting for God, desiring Him. I'm talking about praising and worshipping God despite your situation. Psalm forty-two sheds light on the idea of being spiritually dry or ashy.

Psalm 42:1-8

42 As the hart panteth after the water brooks, so panteth my soul after thee, O God.2 My soul thirsteth for God, for the living God: when shall I come and appear before God?3 My tears have been my meat day and night, while they continually say unto me, Where is thy God?4 When I remember these things, I pour out my soul in me: for I had gone with the multitude, I went with them to the house of God, with the voice of joy and praise, with a multitude that kept holyday.5 Why art thou cast down, O my soul? and why art thou disquieted in me? hope thou in God: for I shall yet praise him for the help of his countenance.6 O my God, my soul is cast down within me: therefore will I remember thee from the land of Jordan, and of the Hermonites, from the hill Mizar.7 Deep calleth unto deep at the noise of thy waterspouts: all thy waves and thy billows are gone over me.8 Yet the LORD will command his loving-kindness in the day time, and in the night his song shall be with me, and my prayer unto the God of my life.

The word pant means to breathe hard and quickly or to say something while you're breathing quickly and heavily. It can also mean to wish for or want something very eagerly. David let us know that he desired God like the dear running for the water brooks. He wanted more of God, even though things in his life were dry. He was going through a bad situation. We must desire more of God in our lives, even in tuff situations. Sometimes it can feel like we're on the mountaintop, but there are valleys too. We must stay hydrated with praise!

Psalm 27:4

4 One thing have I desired of the Lord, that will I seek after; that I may dwell in the house of the LORD all the days of my life, to behold the beauty of the Lord, and to enquire in his temple.

Do we want to worship? Sometimes while running and living for Jesus, we get tired. We're running for Jesus like the deer is running after the water brook. Spiritually sometimes we are taking deep breaths and saying, "I need you to help me, Lord." We have all been there.

David desired to be in the Lord's presence. David was also looking for something. How do we know he was looking for something? The scripture mentions a very keyword and that is the word behold. It means to look or gaze upon the beauty of the Lord. The word beauty translated in Hebrew means favor.

When we worship and desire more of God, we will see His favor in our life. Do we want to worship? Are you thirsty for God? Only God can quench what we need in every area of our lives. God is the thirst quencher. God is the one that ends the drought in our lives. God desires us to worship him and get rid of the spiritual ash in our lives!

God knows all about us. He knows everything you have encountered. Verse three of Psalm forty-two stated, "my tears have been my meat day and night, while they continually say unto me, where is thy God"?

He sees our tears, and He does not ignore them. The Lord has a way of turning things around as we desire Him. People may say, "Where is your God"? However, if you keep a desire for God, he will show up and bless you. The Lord will bless you in front of the people that doubted. Our souls can become cast down when we think God hasn't seen our tears. I want to encourage you that God sees your tears, and He hasn't forgotten about you.

Hebrews 6:10

10 For God is not unrighteous to forget your work and labour of love, which ye have shewed toward his name, in that ye have ministered to the saints, and do minister.

We must keep on living for the Lord when things get tuff. We must keep on ministering to God and His people when things aren't going the way we thought. God has a way of blessing us when we stay faithful.

The Lord will remember us, and be kind to us, as we desire more of Him. We must put our hope in God. A definition of hope is confidence or assurance in the possibility that what one desires or longs for will happen. It can also mean an assurance that expectations will happen. We must put our hope in Christ.

Romans 12:12-13

12. Rejoicing in hope; patient in tribulation; continuing instant in prayer;

13 Distributing to the necessity of saints; given to hospitality.

You must quit getting attitudes, being mean, and jealous, because you're going through something. Don't let your environment make you bitter and spiritually ashy but do just the opposite. We must keep praising God and be patient because God will bring us out. We must remain patient when our faith is tested because Christ is our hope.

Colossians 1:27

27 To whom God would make known what is the riches of the glory of this mystery among the Gentiles; which is Christ in you, the hope of glory:

Psalm 84:11-12

11 For the Lord God is a sun and shield: the Lord will give grace and glory: no good thing will he withhold from them that walk uprightly.12 O Lord of hosts, blessed is the man that trusteth in thee.

Let's look at verse seven of Psalm forty-two. God will continue to quench our spiritual thirst as we long for Him. Do you want more of God? Sometimes God allows challenges even when we are going through. He knows how to get our attention, even when we're going through some waters.

Psalm42:7

7. Deep calleth unto deep at the noise of thy waterspouts: all thy waves and thy billows are gone over me.

Deep water can cause a person to drown. Sometimes we go through some deep stuff, but I want to encourage you Christ is with you. Life will give you stuff you can't explain to other people. However, God is our lifeguard. He will provide, protect, and care for us. Are you ready to stop walking around spiritually ashy? God is ready to show us off, and we can't be walking around looking anyway. We must realize that the Lord desires to use us for his glory. He has need of us!

Chapter 17 The Lord desires to use you

I suffered being poisoned and going through depression, and it was a very trying time in my life. God brought me through it and let me know He was still going to use me. I thought it was over when I was sick, but God showed me He was a Doctor. I began to get back on my feet after God healed me. God blessed me, and I received an opportunity to be a part of a chaplaincy program at a local hospital.

I was like, "wow what a blessing." I had visions of ministering to people that I didn't even know before God opened the opportunity. God was letting me know that he desired to use me. Everything I went through was not in vain. One thing I learned was to have compassion for others because I knew how it felt to be sick.

I hope to encourage someone that God desires to use you for His glory. It doesn't matter what has happened to you, because sometimes bad things happen to good people. However, it doesn't have to be the end of the matter. God can restore, renewing, healing, and saving. There have been a few times in my life where bad things happened to me that I couldn't control. People lied on me. People betrayed me. People stole from me. I struggled why did one of my children have special needs? These things hurt, and I would be lying to say they didn't.

I was able to keep going because God touched my mind. God gave me strength when I wanted to throw in the tile. God brought me up out of that spiritual pit of depression. I felt like, "why is all this stuff happening to me, Lord"? I thought what's going on with my life. Did I do something wrong to you God?

How could this be, and I tried my best to live right and fear the Lord. It's not adding up I thought. I remember pouring my heart and money into a music album. I worked hard on the project and finished it. I pitch it to a record company, who signed me but didn't do anything for me. However, they tried to still my rights to my music. I felt betrayed and used as an artist. I felt like I let myself down and my family. I got depressed didn't want to write anymore. I didn't want to do ministry anymore. I thought to myself stick a fork in me; I'm done!

I was mad at God, to be honest. I thought to myself if you love me, why didn't you help? God let me know that he did, but I didn't listen. I thank God for His mercy, even though the bad things happened. The Lord still loved me and wanted to use me. God wanted me to get over my pity party and stop blaming everybody. God let me know that He would restore me, and He did. He wanted to use me for His glory!

I hope to encourage someone that God desires to use you. He desires to use you in a great way to impact your family and community. God desires to use despite the bad things that have happened to you. The almighty God wants to work through you. You're valuable to God. Sometimes the bad things that have happened to us will hinder how we see ourselves. However, are you ready to be used by God?

God will take what seems like a mess and give us a testimony. God can take years of hurt and abuse and bring healing. God can give us a brand-new start. I needed a brand-new start after those people tried to steal my music. I needed a brand-new start after people lied on me after I had been a blessing to them. We all need another chance, and God isn't stingy on giving out mercy.

Doctor Jesus knows how to come in minister to our broken-ness. He knows how to come in your life and lift you from that depression that's killing you. Doctor Jesus knows how to heal us from the inside out. There is nothing too hard for Him. He knows how to get to the core of our problems and still use us to do great things. Are you ready for God to use you?

It's time to tell the pity party bye! It's time to tell depression bye! It's time to tell low self-esteem bye! It's time to tell your past bye! It's time to tell that divorce bye! It's time to tell rejection bye! It's time to tell all the guilt bye! It's time to tell all the pain bye! It's time to tell all the sorrow bye! God has so much in store for you, and therefore the enemy has fought you so hard.

It's time to forgive yourself of the bad things that happened to you. You couldn't control what happened, so quit beating your-self up. It's time for you to get up and rise to your purpose. God wants to use you. It's time to dry your tears because God has plans for you! The suitcase that's in your closet, please get it out. God is taking you somewhere! The Lord desires to use you!

There is nothing too hard for God. The truth of the matter is, have you considered that God was bragging on you. Have you considered that everything that happened was for a reason? Listen the Bible speaks to us through a man named Job. This man lost everything. He was rich but lost it all. He lost his family to a bad storm. He lost his cattle. He lost his health. This man went through some traumatic things, which most of us will never go through. However, he didn't curse God.

Our bad things don't even compare to the sufferings of Job. However, God was using Job and had a plan for his life. God was bragging on him in heaven, and Job didn't even know it. Sometimes God is bragging on us, and we don't even know it. We've been counted worthy to suffer some things for the glory of God. We must recognize, and that deserves a praise break! The Lord longs to use us even in our pain. Let's look at some scripture to be encouraged along the way.

Job 1:6-12

6 Now there was a day when the sons of God came to present themselves before the Lord, and Satan came also among them.7 And the Lord said unto Satan, Whence comest thou? Then Satan answered the Lord, and said, From going to and fro in the earth, and from walking up and down in it.8 And the Lord said unto Satan, Hast thou considered my servant Job, that there is none like him in the earth, a perfect and an upright man, one that feareth God, and escheweth evil?9 Then Satan answered the Lord, and said, Doth Job fear God for nought?10 Hast not thou made an hedge about him, and about his house, and about all that he hath on every side? thou hast blessed the work of his hands, and his substance is increased in the land.11 But put forth thine hand now, and touch all that he hath, and he will curse thee to thy face.12 And the Lord said unto Satan, Behold, all that he hath is

in thy power; only upon himself put not forth thine hand. So Satan went forth from the presence of the Lord.

God believed in Job and wanted to use him for His glory. God already knew Job wouldn't curse Him or leave Him. God will use someone like that in a mighty way. God can use us in a mighty way; when we have a mindset of truly living for Him in the good and bad times. Job went through so much, but God also gave him double for all his trouble. God knows how to give us back double for all the hurt and pain. The Lord longs to use you for his glory; so, let him have his way in your life.

Luke 19:28-40, 44

28 And when he had thus spoken, he went before, ascending up to Jerusalem.29 And it came to pass, when he was come nigh to Bethphage and Bethany, at the mount called the mount of Olives, he sent two of his disciples,30 Saying, Go ye into the village over against you; in the which at your entering ye shall find a colt tied, whereon yet never man sat: loose him, and bring him hither.31 And if any man ask you, Why do ye loose him? thus shall ye say unto him, Because the Lord hath need of him.32 And they that were sent went their way, and found even as he had said unto them.33 And as they were loosing the colt, the owners thereof said unto them, Why loose ye the colt?34 And they said, The Lord hath need of him.35 And they brought him to Jesus: and they cast their garments upon the colt, and they set Jesus thereon.36 And as he went, they spread their clothes in the way.37 And when he was come nigh, even now at the descent of the mount of Olives,

the whole multitude of the disciples began to rejoice and praise God with a loud voice for all the mighty works that they had seen;38 Saying, Blessed be the King that cometh in the name of the Lord: peace in heaven, and glory in the highest.39 And some of the Pharisees from among the multitude said unto him, Master, rebuke thy disciples.40 And he answered and said unto them, I tell you that, if these should hold their peace, the stones would immediately cry out.

44 And shall lay thee even with the ground, and thy children within thee; and they shall not leave in thee one stone upon another; because thou knewest not the time of thy visitation.

Here in this text, Jesus on his way to Jerusalem. He had corrected his followers on who he was before this. He also had spent time with Zacchaeus and told him to come down from the tree. It was his time of visitation. During this time, He corrects his followers on the true nature of His kingdom. He had to correct them, because of their expectations of who He was to them.

The Jews thought that the coming Messiah would ride in on a stallion horse and deliver them from the Romans. They thought the kingdom of God would appear right then, and immediately. However, Jesus began to correct them, and speak a parable about stewardship until he returns. We see this in Luke chapter nineteen and verse eleven through twenty-seven. Jesus was saying, "I'm getting ready to die, but take care of what I give you." Be a good steward with the gifts that I have given you because I'm coming back.

He spoke a parable unto them about stewardship. I submit a question, are we good steward? God desires to use us, but we must be a good steward over what He has given us. We must be a good steward over the gifts, talents, resources, and money He has given us. We must be a good steward over our families.

Jesus and his followers at that point had unrealistic expectations because they didn't understand who He was. They didn't understand that He was about to die, but Christ knew He was about to die. He was a wanted man. He was not going to kill the Romans, but He was going to die for the sins of humanity. He speaks the parable, and then the Bible declares he goes up to Jerusalem. He knew the cross was coming.

God desires to use you but there's a cross to bear. We must bear our cross if God is going to use us. It's a price to pay, but it will be worth it. Maybe the bad things that happened to you were a part of your cross, but God is going to get some glory out of it.

Christians view the cross as a cherished symbol of atonement, forgiveness, grace, and love. However, in Jesus' day, the cross represented nothing but a torturous and agonizing death. The Romans forced convicted criminals to carry their crosses to the place of crucifixion. When a person carried their cross; it meant carrying their execution device while facing ridicule along the way to death. My brother, my sister, maybe you had to face some ridicule along the way. I hope to inspire you that it's not over until God says it's over!

The scripture stated, "Take up your cross and follow me." We must be willing to die to self. It's a call to absolute surrender. After each time Jesus commanded cross-bearing, He said, "For whoever wants to save his life will lose it, but whoever loses his life for me will save it. The Word declares, "what good is it for a man to gain the whole world, and yet lose or forfeit his very self?" (Luke 9:24-25).

The call is tough, but the reward is matchless. Our self-will must die, so God's will can come alive in our lives. Please remember that the Lord desires to use you! We must quit thinking we know it all and rely on God and the Word. Quit trying to do everything your way and do it God's way. It's time to surrender. Peace, joy, favor, and the comfort of the Holy Spirit will come upon us; when we surrender to God desires for us. Are you ready to be used by God?

Jesus is a wanted man in this text. He knows people have rejected Him. He knows people want to kill Him, but He is on His way. He arrived at the Mount of Olives and told two of His disciples to go into the village. Jesus told them they would find a colt they would have to untie him. This colt no man had ever been on Him. It was a young colt, not old. Jesus wanted the young horse that had no experience. God had it prearranged, and no one had been on the colt. The seat was for Jesus and Jesus only. Jesus said, "When you find the colt untie him, loose him."

My next point I want to share with you is; the Lord is freeing you up. God is releasing you because he desires to use you! Why did he need the colt? He needed the colt because the Word of God was getting ready to be fulfilled. God is going to fulfill His precious promises in your life but are you ready? Are you ready to take a ride with the Master?

Zechariah 9:9

Rejoice greatly, O daughter of Zion; shout, O daughter of Jerusalem: behold, thy King cometh unto thee: he is just, and having salvation; lowly, and riding upon an ass, and upon a colt the foal of an ass.

He is releasing you to do His will. He has spoken over our lives, and things will come to pass. We may be experiencing trouble, pain, a setback, but God wants to use us. God knows how to bring a release into our lives. I don't know about you, but I receive my release. A release that empowers us to do His will and purpose for our lives. It's time to be released. You've been tied up too long, and God wants to set you free from that situation. When a person is tied up, it's hard to be used by God. Everybody will not understand why God is bringing a release in your life. Some people don't want to see you free, but God desires that we be free, and not tied down in bondage.

Luke19:31-34

31 And if any man ask you, Why do ye loose him? thus shall ye say unto him, Because the Lord hath need of him.32 And they that were sent went their way, and found even as he had said unto them.33 And as they were loosing the colt, the owners thereof said unto them, Why loose ye the colt?34 And they said, The Lord hath need of him.

Matthew 21:2

2. Saying unto them, Go into the village over against you, and straightway ye shall find an ass tied, and a colt with her: loose them, and bring them unto me.

Matthew's account of this same story puts the colt there and the colt's mother. However, Jesus did not get on the donkey but rode on the colt. Donkeys have a reputation for being stubborn animals. This reputation has come from a common misunderstanding of the differences between the behavior of donkeys and horses. Donkeys seem to have an element of self-preservation and are unwilling to do anything that might be dangerous.

Jesus chooses the young colt and not the stubborn mother to ride into a dangerous situation. I'm trying to tell you; that God doesn't need us to be stubborn but to be willing. Are you willing to follow God? Are you willing to be used by God?

Isaiah 1:19-20

19 If ye be willing and obedient, ye shall eat the good of the land:20 But if ye refuse and rebel, ye shall be devoured with the sword: for the mouth of the Lord hath spoken it.

1 Samuel 15:22-24

22 And Samuel said, Hath the Lord as great delight in burnt offerings and sacrifices, as in obeying the voice of the Lord? Behold, to obey is better than sacrifice, and to hearken than the fat of rams.23 For rebellion is as the sin of witchcraft, and stubbornness is as iniquity and idolatry. Because thou hast rejected the

word of the Lord, he hath also rejected thee from being king.24 And Saul said unto Samuel, I have sinned: for I have transgressed the commandment of the Lord, and thy words: because I feared the people, and obeyed their voice.

We must decrease and let God increase even more in our lives. The more we let God have His way in our lives, we will see positive results. We will see Him for who He is in our lives. We will discover that God is true and faithful. We will know that He is a provider and a promise keeper. We will know that He is a protector, sustainer, healer, and our Savior. We will know that God doesn't lie.

God deserves praise because He has you covered. The Bible mentioned before they set Jesus on the colt. They put garments on the colt. They covered him, and then Jesus set on him. We must keep Christ first and allow Him to use us. He will cover us. He will cover us in His blood. He will cover us with His protection. He will cover us with favor. He will cover us with grace, and mercy. They covered the colt, and Jesus was in position. They began to pay homage to the Savior. They began to give him praise.

Luke 19: 35-38

35. And they brought him to Jesus: and they cast their garments upon the colt, and they set Jesus thereon.36 And as he went, they spread their clothes in the way.37 And when he was come nigh, even now at the descent of the mount of Olives, the whole multitude of the disciples began to rejoice and praise God with a loud voice for all the mighty works that they had seen;38

Saying, Blessed be the King that cometh in the name of the Lord: peace in heaven, and glory in the highest.

We must understand when God chooses us, and it may not be easy. We may be going through some things but count it all joy. You may be untried and never been this way before, but he knows it's your time of visitation. God is ready to visit you and bless you. It's your time. It's your time; that's why some things didn't work out because God has something better. It's your time, that's why the enemy has fought you so hard.

James 1:2-3

2 My brethren, count it all joy when ye fall into divers temptations;3 Knowing this, that the trying of your faith worketh patience.

The religious people of that day missed it because they thought it was about them. They thought they knew everything. They were full of hate towards Jesus because of whom he chose. Don't be surprised if you feel hate and jealousy as you walk in your purpose. It comes with the territory.

Luke 19:39-40, 44

39. And some of the Pharisees from among the multitude said unto him, Master, rebuke thy disciples.40 And he answered and said unto them, I tell you that, if these should hold their peace, the stones would immediately cry out. 44 And shall lay thee even with the ground, and thy children within thee; and they shall not leave

in thee one stone upon another; because thou knewest not the time of thy visitation.

Don't let haters or doubters stop you because the Lord desires to use you. There is a blessing on the other side. Don't miss your time because of distractions. Don't miss your time because of fear, but let God use you. There is nothing like being in the center of God's will for your life. Let God use you so he can rebuild your life!

Chapter 18 Let God rebuild your life

Christ is a master carpenter. Christ will rebuild your life if you let Him. I remember growing up as a child, and I always wanted to go to my grandparents' house. They always had good food. They would let us eat whatever we wanted. My grandfather had a garden. He took good care of it. He would let us work in the garden during the summertime, but he always showed us what to do first. I love working in the garden with him and my dad. He would also pay me something too.

He also had a shotgun, which he kept just in case. We didn't touch that gun, and everybody knew it was his. We used to be like, "don't touch that gun or granddaddy is going to get you." We knew it was off limits. However, you could see it standing up behind his old dresser. I saw him pull it out one time when he was mad. Everybody ran out of the house, but I'm glad he didn't shoot anyone that day! I had a lot of great memories at that house.

One thing that stuck out about that house was the outdoor shed. My granddaddy called it the little house. This shed was where he staged his equipment for the garden. He also used it to house his tools. He had so many tools consisting of wrenches, saws, pliers, saw table, and many other tools. I remember he would cut wood and other things in that shed. He was great at building things. He had bought his land and built his own house. He was a carpenter, but he never really bragged about it.

However, I remember when I got saved. I was staying with my grandfather. I remember having a vision. The Lord showed me that little house and the tools. God began to reveal to me that He was going to rebuild my life. I knew I had to work the tools that He gave me. God knows how to rebuild our lives from the ground up. He knows how to rebuild us, even if it means we must start over.

Sometimes life will give you a bad hand. The Lord knows how to rebuild and give you a better life. He knows how to guide you, and inspire you, to use the tools or gifts that He has placed in you. God is a master builder, the great carpenter! We can trust Him to build our lives because He has the master plan. He desires that we follow him and let his master plan unfold in our lives.

My life started badly in my early twenties, but God rebuilt me. I hope to encourage someone that God knows how to rebuild, where you messed up. God knows how to rebuild when there has been opposition. God knows how to rebuild and make something out of you, that will leave people baffled. Don't throw in the tile but let God work on you.

The Lord can rebuild us, where we have experienced depression, abuse, rejection, and low self-esteem. We must learn to get out of the way and let him work. My granddaddy would tell us to get out of the way; when we didn't know what to with the tools. He didn't want us to get hurt so that he would give us instruction. He taught us how to handle the tools.

God doesn't want to see us hurt either. Sometimes we don't know what to do, with what God has given us. The Lord knows how to take charge and show us what to do and provide instructions. When He gives instructions, we must listen. We can be effective with the tools He has given us if we listen.

Bad things happen to good people, but we serve an able God. He will take our spiritual mess and turn things around. God knows how to rebuild lives as we see in the Bible. God helped his people rebuild the wall and the temple. God moved upon his people when things looked beyond repair. He inspired them to start the process of rebuilding. God will inspire or motivate us to stand up. It's not over until God says it's over. Let's look at an example in the Word of God.

Ezra 5:1-5

Then the prophets, Haggai the prophet, and Zechariah the son of Iddo, prophesied unto the Jews that were in Judah and Jerusalem in the name of the God of Israel, even unto them.2 Then rose up Zerubbabel the son of Shealtiel, and Jeshua the son of Jozadak, and began to build the house of God which is at Jerusalem: and with them were the prophets of God helping them.3 At the same time came to them Tatnai, governor on this side the river, and Shetharboznai and their companions, and said thus unto them, Who hath commanded you to build this house, and to make up this wall?4 Then said we unto them after this manner, What are the names of the men that make this building?5 But the eye of their God was upon the elders of the Jews, that they could not cause them to cease, till the matter came to Darius: and then they returned answer by letter concerning this matter.

Here in this text, the Jews went into exile in 586 BC. They were taken into captivity in Babylon by King Nebuchadnezzar. He also destroyed the temple that Solomon built during this time. Nebuchadnezzar went into the House of God and took the gold, silver, and treasury from the House of God. It looked like all hope was lost, but God began to do a new thing in 539BC.

God began to restore or rebuild the lives of His people and His temple. God used another king, by the name of Cyrus to defeat Nebuchadnezzar. He defeated him. Cyrus then made a decree being God's anointed to set the people of God free. He set them free, so they go back home to Jerusalem. They were free to start the process of rebuilding. God wanted the temple, the city, and the lives of the people rebuilt. When God is rebuilding something or someone, no one can stop Him.

The Book of Ezra reveals to us how the people arrived back home after exile. However, about two years later, they began to rebuild the house of God. We see this in chapter three. They laid the foundation and began to celebrate, but the celebration is short-lived. Opposition from their enemies caused the process to come to a screeching halt, at first. Their enemies hated on their rebuilding process.

We find in chapter four, a group of people stirred up trouble. These people had no right to what God had decreed. However, they began to come against the people of God. They decided they wanted to be a part of it. God's people said no. The people, who were told no, at that point began to oppose them. They lied on them and discourage them. They oppose them, so much that they lied on the people to the king. They lied that the people of God were building to take over them, and the king. It was a lie to stop the progress of God's people. The lie didn't work. God would vindicate his people. The people of God were trying to be obedient to God in this story.

We must understand that some people will not be happy about God rebuilding your life. People will lie and try to hinder your progress, just like this story in the Bible. You must hold on to the promises of God. God will not fail you. He will not lie! The lie appeared to have work for a season because the king had the work stopped. The people lost their confidence. My friends, we can outlive a lie. Sometimes you have been through things and opposition. However, you must get your confidence back so that you can continue with your spiritual renovations.

I notice something in the text that may help us in our process. We can't forget about what God has spoken over our lives. Chapter five, no one said what God had already decreed or ordained through Cyrus. They allowed all the lying, frustration, disappointment, setbacks, and opposition to deceive them. They forgot what God had already ordained. Don't let life make you forget who you are; and what God has spoken about you.

God had already declared that they were free. He decreed that they could rebuild the temple. He gave them divine authority. The people of God didn't say anything about the decree when the opposition came. God can rebuild our lives after the storm. God can rebuild our lives after we have been down for so long. God can rebuild our lives if we believe him and take him at His Word. God can make things better, but don't forget about what God has already spoken about you! Sometimes we must remind others and ourselves. He is watching over us and his Word to perform it.

Ezra chapter five, God used two prophets to get the people's focus on Him. Haggai was the prophet that said, "Consider your ways." How is it that God house sits in ruin and you're not concern about it? God used him to bring His people into accountability and conviction. We must have our priorities in order when God is rebuilding our lives (Haggai 1). God must be first!

Sometimes we wonder why things don't work out in our lives or our process. Could it be you have God second, third, fourth, or fifth in your life? You could be making money only to put it into your pockets, that have holes in it. God's people were like this in the book of Ezra. However, they made up in their minds, that they were going to start rebuilding. A turn around happened after that!

Zechariah, the other prophet in Ezra chapter five dealt with repentance and not despising small beginnings. Zechariah let the people know it was not just about the building. It was about the people going to the building, and that they needed to repent. They needed to be encouraged. God was going to care for them.

Zechariah 4:9-10

9 The hands of Zerubbabel have laid the foundation of this house; his hands shall also finish it; and thou shalt know that the Lord of hosts hath sent me unto you.

10 For who hath despised the day of small things? for they shall rejoice and shall see the plummet in the hand of Zerubbabel with those seven; they are the eyes of the Lord, which run to and fro through the whole earth.

God was saying I started this work, and I'm going to finish it. The Word of God lets us know we should not despise small or humble beginnings when God is rebuilding our lives. They listen to the prophets in Ezra, chapter five. They started rebuilding again, but this time they didn't stop when opposition came. The people of God kept building because they remembered what God said through his prophets. They remembered what God had said through Cyrus. This time they told them what God said; and made them bring back the report (Ezra 5:5-17).

Ezra 6:1-10

1. Then Darius the king made a decree, and search was made in the house of the rolls, where the treasures were laid up in Babylon.2 And there was found at Achmetha, in the palace that is in the province of the Medes, a roll, and therein was a record thus written:3 In the first year of Cyrus the king the same Cyrus the king made a decree concerning the house of God at Jerusalem, Let the house be builded, the place where they offered sacrifices, and let the foundations thereof be strongly laid; the height thereof threescore cubits, and the breadth thereof threescore cubits;4 With three rows of great stones, and a row of new timber: and let the expenses be given out of the king's house:5 And also let the golden and silver vessels of the house of God, which Nebuchadnezzar took forth out of the temple which is at Jerusalem, and brought unto Babylon, be restored, and brought again unto the temple which is at Jerusalem, everyone to his place, and place them in the house of God.6 Now therefore, Tatnai, governor beyond the river, Shetharboznai, and your companions the

Apharsachites, which are beyond the river, be ye far from thence:7 Let the work of this house of God alone; let the governor of the Jews and the elders of the Jews build this house of God in his place.8 Moreover I make a decree what ye shall do to the elders of these Jews for the building of this house of God: that of the king's goods, even of the tribute beyond the river, forthwith expenses be given unto these men, that they be not hindered.9 And that which they have need of, both young bullocks, and rams, and lambs, for the burnt offerings of the God of heaven, wheat, salt, wine, and oil, according to the appointment of the priests which are at Jerusalem, let it be given them day by day without fail. 10 That they may offer sacrifices of sweet savours unto the God of heaven, and pray for the life of the king, and of his sons.

God has a record. God knows what He has spoken over our lives, and He cannot lie. God doesn't forget. My brother, my sister, God, will not forget about you! We might forget, but God doesn't forget. He remembers what He has promised to us. God has a record of all that we have done for Him.

God made those people find what He said and decreed by Cyrus. He made them search and find it. The people were searching, and the Israelites were building while they were searching. Sometimes we must keep working while God fixed things and situations in our lives. The people found the decree after a long search. God is working behind the scenes for our good. Don't quit but keep using your tools, because God knows how to rebuild your life!

Ephesians 2:10

10 For we are his workmanship, created in Christ Jesus unto good works, which God hath before ordained that we should walk in them.

God has people looking, searching to bless us. They may not even understand why they are doing it, but God has ordained for us to bear fruit. He will touch people hearts to bless us. The Lord knows how to touch people in high places to give us favor. God has someone looking to bless you!

Proverbs 21:1

1. The king's heart is in the hand of the Lord, as the rivers of water: he turneth it whithersoever he will.

We find in chapter six of Ezra that they found the decree. They reported back to the king what they found. What they found is what God said through Cyrus, which was let my people go and let them rebuild the temple. Darius, the new king, basically said, "give them back what was taking out of the house of God." God will give us back what the devil thought he took and more. You thought you were losing, but God was setting you up for the victory. God deserves praise!

This time after the king and the people saw the report, and it changed everything. They knew then we better leave these people along. I'm paraphrasing, but King Darius said, "leave them alone, give them the finances to rebuild, and everything they need to rebuild." God turned that thing around for His people because He had made a promise.

The favor of God is on display in chapter six of Ezra. God has favor for you and your purpose. It's a great work but remember what God has decreed in your life. The people of God received a double blessing. The government paid for the rebuilding of the temple. They didn't have to pay for it. They also supplied them with what they needed daily. Jesus is rebuilding our lives. He is the great carpenter, let Him work! God knows how to rebuild our lives.

Isaiah 61: 7

7. For your shame ye shall have double; and for confusion they shall rejoice in their portion: therefore in their land they shall possess the double: everlasting joy shall be unto them.

Philippians 4:19

19. But my God shall supply all your need according to his riches in glory by Christ Jesus.

I hope you're ready to receive the life that God has for you. A life where you trust God because He never lies, and we can depend on Him. Do you know who you are? We're king's kids, and we deserve the best, so let Him rebuild your life. He knows what is best for us. You can rest knowing everything He promised will come to pass. Please remember numbers twenty-three and nineteen!

Chapter 19 Invest in you

Music has always been a part of my life going back to elementary school. I recall playing in the orchestra. I played the viola, but I was not exactly great at it and needed a lot of practice. My family couldn't afford to buy me and my sister a viola back then, but the school let us use theirs. I started learning to play, and it was hard at first. My instructor encouraged me to keep practicing and take our lessons seriously. My instructor wanted me to buy into practicing and using my gift of music.

She saw something in me that I didn't see because I was so young. She was saying if you become great at what you do, it could become a blessing in your life. She knew it. She had traveled around a lot performing music. She knew what it took.

I look back on it now; it was as if she was saying, "Invest in your gift." We must learn to invest in ourselves! God has put in every one of us gifts and talents. We must use those gifts because God is looking for a return on His investment. He put those gifts in us so that we would use them for His glory. He put them in us to be a blessing to us but also for others.

A tree bears fruit not for itself but the enjoyment of others. God has put some great stuff in us. He wants others to see it, and possibly be inspired by our gifts. God will take care of us and bless us as we used the gift. We must learn to invest in us; because when we function in what God has chosen us to do life is so much better. God means for us to use those talents and gifts.

I've learned to invest in what God has put in me. Let me share an example. I love to write and preach the Word of God. I invested in myself because I believe God put that gift of preaching in me. I believe He chose me to do it. I went to school to learn more in-depth about the Bible. I wanted to preach with the spirit of excellence. Did it cost me a lot of money? The answer is yes! However, God has blessed me in ministry.

I have been able to travel to different states and preach the Gospel. I have been able to preach in my hometown, and it helped people. God continues to bless and expand me as I operate in my gift. There is a blessing in investing in you. God desires that we invest in what He has given us. We must learn that it is fine to believe and love ourselves. God has so much for you when you embrace that about yourself. It took me a while to learn that, but now I know. I have seen God's hand bless me because I invested in what He gave me. God has no respect of person He will do it for you as well.

You must know your value and worth, and not what people think is your value and worth. God may put something in you is so valuable. You must take advantage of that opportunity and work it. God is looking for a return on His investment in you. Don't fear but invest in you. Don't fear to believe in you! Let us look at the power of investing in the Word of God.

Ecclesiastes 11:1-5

11 Cast thy bread upon the waters: for thou shalt find it after many days.2 Give a portion to seven, and also to eight; for thou knowest not what evil shall be upon the earth.3 If the clouds be

full of rain, they empty themselves upon the earth: and if the tree fall toward the south, or toward the north, in the place where the tree falleth, there it shall be.4 He that observeth the wind shall not sow; and he that regardeth the clouds shall not reap.5 As thou knowest not what is the way of the spirit, nor how the bones do grow in the womb of her that is with child: even so thou knowest not the works of God who maketh all.

We must invest and let God bring us a great return! We are to use our resources and opportunities wisely. When God has blessed us or has given us resources, we should, at some point, invest in them. God has given us also businesses and incomes. My brothers, my sisters, invest in you!

Some commentators believe Solomon was referring to ships when he said, "cast thy bread upon the waters." Solomon sent out ships and was involved in trading. These ships came back with gold and silver. These ships came back with goods from trading with other countries. One can only imagine that the ships went through a lot. The ships and the people had to endure storms. They had to endure perhaps sickness and violent waves and winds. However, they kept going. Some perhaps didn't make it, but it appears they had success. It may have taken them weeks or months to see their return on their investments, but they invested.

2 Chronicles 8:18

18 And Huram sent him by the hands of his servants' ships, and servants that had knowledge of the sea; and they went with

the servants of Solomon to Ophir and took thence four hundred and fifty talents of gold, and brought them to king Solomon.

1 Kings 9:26-27

26. And King Solomon made a navy of ships in Eziongeber, which is beside Eloth, on the shore of the Red Sea, in the land of Edom.27 And Hiram sent in the navy his servants, shipmen that had knowledge of the sea, with the servants of Solomon.

He was describing an investment that will come back to us, particularly in troubled times. Therefore, we are not to withhold giving of our gifts, talents, resources, and ourselves. King Solomon was referring to a person being faithful in what God has given you. You must keep going and not give up because investing in you is worth it. We must stay faithful and believe even in rough times.

We must stay faithful and trust that the process or the investment is going to pay off. We must be patient. It is in our patience that we obtain what God has for us. We can take money in the natural and invest in the stock market. We must have patience and let the investment work for us. A great return doesn't happen overnight in most cases in the stock market. We must have patience when we invest in our gifts, talents, and resources.

Hebrews 6:11-15

11 And we desire that every one of you do shew the same diligence to the full assurance of hope unto the end: 12 That ye be

not slothful, but followers of them who through faith and patience inherit the promises.13 For when God made promise to Abraham, because he could swear by no greater, he sware by himself,14 Saying, Surely blessing I will bless thee, and multiplying I will multiply thee.15 And so, after he had patiently endured, he obtained the promise.

When we invest in what God has told us to do, we will obtain what He has for us. We must carry on my friends. We must carry on and be prepared. We must be practical. Sometimes bad things happen, and we can't change people. We can't change everything that has happened to us, because it may have been out of our control. However, we can change our attitude.

It is what it is! All we can control is how we respond if something bad has happened to us. When we encounter evil and unexpected storms that Solomon said, "we must carry on." We also must be prepared." We must stay faithful. When we keep going, we carry on like a good soldier. God has a way of taking us to another level in him. Verse two of this text helps us to understand.

Ecclesiastes 11:2

2 Give a portion to seven, and to eight; for thou knowest not what evil shall be upon the earth.

As we prepare ourselves now with the opportunities, talents, and resources; it will help provide protection and comfort when bad days come. We need to make the most of what we have now and prepare for our future. Who knows what tomorrow holds? We still must prepare if God lets us see it. We must be prepared by investing and believing in ourselves. There is a reason God wants us to press on.

The Bible declares before Esther could have a night with the king, which would change her life and her people. She had to be ready to walk in her purpose. I could only imagine Ester believe in herself and what God put in her. She took advantage of her resources that were around her. We, too, must take advantage of the resources God has put around us. It will help us receive a great return from God.

God can give us a great return if we invest in our selves. He is looking for a great return on His investment anyway. Does it mean everything will happen overnight? The answer is no. However, we must believe that our return on investment will surely come.

Esther 2:12-17

12 Now when every maid's turn was come to go in to king Ahasuerus, after that she had been twelve months, according to the manner of the women, (for so were the days of their purifications accomplished, to wit, six months with oil of myrrh, and six months with sweet odours, and with other things for the purifying of the women;)13 Then thus came every maiden unto the king; whatsoever she desired was given her to go with her out of the house of the women unto the king's house.14 In the evening she went, and on the morrow she returned into the second house of the women, to the custody of Shaashgaz, the king's chamberlain, which kept the concubines: she came in unto the king no more, except the king delighted in her, and that she were called by name.15 Now when the turn of Esther, the daughter of Abihail

the uncle of Mordecai, who had taken her for his daughter, was come to go in unto the king, she required nothing but what Hegai the king's chamberlain, the keeper of the women, appointed. And Esther obtained favour in the sight of all them that looked upon her.16 So Esther was taken unto king Ahasuerus into his house royal in the tenth month, which is the month Tebeth, in the seventh year of his reign.17 And the king loved Esther above all the women, and she obtained grace and favour in his sight more than all the virgins; so that he set the royal crown upon her head, and made her queen instead of Vashti.

Esther did what they ask her to do. She listened to her mentor. When God is preparing us, we must listen to other people. God will use people to help prepare us for what He has for us. Not only did she do what they asked, but she kept her mouth shut. She didn't reveal who she was until it was time for her to talk. Sometimes we must learn to be quiet because God is preparing us for greatness. God has great things for us. He knows that once you have invested in yourself. He desires to give us a great return, but we must walk in wisdom. It's going to be worth investing in you.

We walk by faith and not by sight. We can't be trick by what we see all the time. Solomon gives us wisdom as we walk on our journey, believing in what we have invested. Let us look at verses three and four.

Ecclesiastes 11:3-4

3. If the clouds be full of rain, they empty themselves upon the earth: and if the tree fall toward the south, or toward the north,

in the place where the tree falleth, there it shall be.4 He that observeth the wind shall not sow; and he that regardeth the clouds shall not reap.

Solomon was perhaps saying, "I have to walk by faith, not by sight." What we see in the natural might trick us. Sometimes we interpret resistance, pain, or a setback as a sign we should stop. Solomon writes about storms causing trees to come crashing down (Ecclesiastes 11:3). When we come across giant trees blocking our path, do we turn back or do we go around, and continue pressing ahead? Don't let that spiritual tree stop you.

The truth of the matter is things will come against us, but that doesn't mean God isn't going to bless you. God is faithful, and He will give you a great return on your investment. We must Don't let situations deceive you when you know God has promised you a great return. My friends invest in you, believe in you!

Solomon tells us the way to apply wisdom in this situation is to quit waiting for everything to be favorable. Everything will not be perfect when investing in you or what God has for you. Everything will not always look favorable, but that doesn't mean you stop working towards the goal. Quit worrying about the winds and clouds and do what God has told you to do. God is looking for our obedience, even if things don't look right.

When you keep looking at what's going on around you, it sometimes discourages you. Don't depend on what you see but what God has spoken. Don't miss opportunities, returns on investments, blessings, and a better life, because you want everything lined up right. It doesn't work like that.

Our circumstances may look bleak today, but they are not signs of what God is doing in the spiritual realm or an indicator of the future. God used Solomon to tell us that our present circumstances are not always a correct interpretation of the future. We should not allow fear to stop us. God wants us to disregard the clouds. Don't worry about the clouds, get rid of these spiritual clouds. They could be holding us back or hindering us. The clouds called fear, doubt, anger, pride, and rejection.

Ecclesiastes 11:5

5 As thou knowest not what is the way of the spirit, nor how the bones do grow in the womb of her that is with child: even so thou knowest not the works of God who maketh all.

We don't know how it's all going to happen or how God will work it out. The Word of God in this scripture gives light. It lets us know that after we have done what God has told us to do, let him give us the results. We are to trust Him and walk in obedience, not disobedience.

God is our sunshine. God will begin to shine in our lives if we put it in his hands for the results for the return. No matter how long it's been raining in our life with trials, setbacks, disappointment, and rejection; God can shine through all the storms of life. We will begin to see his favor upon our lives. When we see His favor upon our lives, that's God's way of smiling at us. I don't know about you, but I want God to smile at me.

Numbers 6:22-27

22. And the Lord spake unto Moses, saying, 23 Speak unto Aaron and unto his sons, saying, On this wise ye shall bless the children of Israel, saying unto them,24 The Lord bless thee, and keep thee:25 The Lord make his face shine upon thee, and be gracious unto thee:26 The Lord lift up his countenance upon thee, and give thee peace.27 And they shall put my name upon the children of Israel, and I will bless them.

Psalm 80:1-7

1. Give ear, O Shepherd of Israel, thou that leadest Joseph like a flock; thou that dwellest between the cherubims, shine forth.2 Before Ephraim and Benjamin and Manasseh stir up thy strength, and come and save us.3 Turn us again, O God, and cause thy face to shine; and we shall be saved.4 O Lord God of hosts, how long wilt thou be angry against the prayer of thy people?5 Thou feedest them with the bread of tears; and givest them tears to drink in great measure.6 Thou makest us a strife unto our neighbours: and our enemies laugh among themselves.7 Turn us again, O God of hosts, and cause thy face to shine; and we shall be saved.

God is turning it around for us. God can restore us and bless us with a great return. God can turn it again and give us a great hand for that bad hand. He is able. Do you believe it, my friends? It's working for our good! My brother, my sisters invest in you!

Genesis 50:20

20. But as for you, ye thought evil against me; but God meant it unto good, to bring to pass, as it is this day, to save much people alive.

There are better days ahead, and God deserves praise and worship. God will give a great return on our investments. Do you believe it? Are you ready to invest in you?

Chapter 20 Keep your confidence in the Lord

I can honestly say I have enjoyed my journey with Christ, my family, friends, and loved ones. It hasn't always been easy. I have my share of pain, setbacks, and made some bad decisions. However, the Lord has seen me through every time. God is so faithful. He never lies. We can have confidence knowing that He will never lie to us. God's words don't fall to the ground. My brothers, my sisters, keep your confidence in the Lord.

I think back on what my grandmother told me how God would use me. I think back on what other preachers told me how God would use me. He has done just that. I say all that not to brag but to show you that God never lies. When God makes a promise to you keep your confidence in him! It's going to pay off in a great way.

God has brought me from a long way. It has been a process learning to trust Him and take Him at His word. However, God continues to show His self-mighty in my life. When people said I would never make in ministry. God has held to His promises, and I am making it. I have become a pastor, as well. I've started a ministry with the blessing of my bishop, but most of all, God's blessings. He continues to do great things and guess what He will do it for you!

I remember growing up as a teenager, and I had confidence as a basketball player; because I use to shoot hoop at neighborhood courts. I didn't know back then who I would become. However, I learn from that time in my life. I remember playing ball at Textile, and King Forest courts. The ball would go through the basketball rim. The chains attached would make that sound, letting you know you just scored. I played in the hood, and we didn't have nets we had chains attached to the rims. I loved playing twenty-one with my homeboys or running full court with them. It brought out a competitive spirit in us, I believe. I know it made me competitive.

It made me want to be the best at hooping, but I wasn't. I had some skills, though. Sometimes it got so competitive people talked trash to each other. I even saw people get into fights over a game of basketball. When I was coming up, I love to splash a jumper in your face and tell you about it! My favorite line was "get down" if you tried to block my shot and I scored.

My older brother worked with me on shooting my jumper going into my first year in high school. He helped me develop my shooting mechanics. I listen to him because he was a successful high school basketball player. He encouraged me that I could do it and get good at it. He helped develop my confidence. I needed that at that time.

I became pretty good at shooting threes before my senior season. My peers knew I had a jump shot. My coaches encourage me to shoot, as well. I had become very confident with my shooting. I felt like I could shoot with the best of them because of my confidence. I have learned to have confidence in what you do, can take you a long way.

I say all that to say you can do great things; if you have confidence in what you do. However, let's take even further. We must have confidence in God most of all, and confidence in ourselves. After all, it is God who made us and gave us talents and gifts. Isn't God amazing? We must keep our confidence in him to do great things through us.

I know what it is to struggle with low self-esteem. I had my times when I didn't see my value because of how I grew up. I had my times when people rejected me. I had my times when I was scared to do things that were out of my comfort zone. However, my relationship helped me overcome those things. God helped me to have confidence away from the basketball court.

When I started to understand that God was all-knowing, all seeing, all powerful, and no one could stop Him. I was like, "I'm putting my trust and confidence in Him no matter what". He will not disappoint. He is trustworthy. He never lies as humanity does. Yes, my friends this why we put our confidence in Him.

I used to be so scared to step out and do things outside of my comfort zone. I was walking in fear because I was scared to fail. I was scared people would talk about if I failed. Well, I have learned that people are going to talk about you anyway. They will talk about if you succeed or fail.

I have learned in my walk with the Lord; it's fine to come from your comfort zone. It's a good thing to step out and do things that you didn't think you could do. It's fine to do those things once you have prayed about it, and God has given you the green light. My friends have confidence that God is going to do great things in your life, family, and community.

It wasn't easy for me at first to have confidence in my writing. It developed over time. I recall in 1995 writing rhymes and poetry. I would let a few people look at, and they were like that's a gift. I was like how I can get better at it; when I don't have the finances and resources to become great at it. The spring of 1997, I started praying about it. God told me to trust Him and let Him lead me in the process.

God started opening doors for me to go to the studio to record. He introduced me to people that were writers. They gave me constructive criticism that would make me a better writer. I started going to workshop and events because I wanted to be great at what I do. I had to step out and keep my confidence in God. I had to keep my confidence because there were times I went through rejection. I knew God had put something in me that was worth keeping!

We must maintain our confidence even when it looks like we shouldn't. We must stick in there with God when things get rough. God is with us on the mountaintop, as well as in the valley. Don't switch on God but keep trusting him. The Word of God let's know we should keep our confidence in God.

Psalm 63

63 O God, thou art my God; early will I seek thee: my soul thirsteth for thee, my flesh longeth for thee in a dry and thirsty land, where no water is;2 To see thy power and thy glory, so as I have seen thee in the sanctuary.3 Because thy loving-kindness is better than life, my lips shall praise thee.4 Thus will I bless thee while I live: I will lift up my hands in thy name.5 My soul shall be satisfied as with marrow and fatness; and my mouth shall praise thee with joyful lips:6 When I remember thee upon my bed, and meditate on thee in the night watches.7 Because thou hast been

my help, therefore in the shadow of thy wings will I rejoice.8 My soul followed hard after thee: thy right hand upholdeth me.9 But those that seek my soul, to destroy it, shall go into the lower parts of the earth.10 They shall fall by the sword: they shall be a portion for foxes.11 But the king shall rejoice in God; every one that sweareth by him shall glory: but the mouth of them that speak lies shall be stopped.

We used to play a game called hide and seek as children. One person started the game off by counting to a certain number. The person's eyes were closed, and they were facing away from the people going to hide. They counted out loud to a certain number. The person came looking for the people that were hiding after counting. The first person caught hiding had to be the next person counting and seeking.

I submit to you fellow believers we have an enemy called the devil who is seeking to destroy God's people. Yes, we are to keep our confidence, but sometimes we must hide spiritually. We must hide because the devil is seeking to destroy our character, our bodies, our families, and our communities. He is seeking to destroy any way he can. However, we as God's people must learn that sometimes we have to hide in God. We must hide because sometimes the battle is too strong for us. When we hide in God, He will protect and preserve us from the plots and schemes of the enemy.

Here in Psalm sixty-three David is on the run and is hiding. He is hiding in the wilderness of Judah. Scholars believe he is either hiding from King Saul, but most scholars believe that he is on the run and hiding from his son Absalom. David is hiding from the son he raised and blessed. Sometimes betrayal comes from the people we love the most. Absalom betrays the king because he wanted to be the king.

The situation drives David and his people away from the palace and into a wilderness. David was a man of God. He kept his confidence in God. Sometimes bad things happen to good people. Sometimes people want what you have, so being used by the devil, they seek to bring you harm. When believers encounter problems like this, we must put our trust in God. We must hide in Him. We must keep our confidence in the Lord.

There are times we must be quiet and hide until God moves for us. David had to be quiet and hide because if he didn't, Absalom could have killed him. It was some hiding and seeking going on. David would eventually win this game, because of his confidence in God. David had a lot of people against him, but God favored him in the situation. The odds may be against you but keep your confidence because victory is coming!

Isaiah 30:15

15 For thus saith the Lord God, the Holy One of Israel; In returning and rest shall ye be saved; in quietness and in confidence shall be your strength: and ye would not.

We don't have to respond to everything the enemy throws at us. It's a blessing to be quiet, don't respond. Let the enemy think what he may, but trust and obey. God is up to something. He knows how to stop the enemy and his tactics.

Proverbs 18:6-7

6 A fool's lips enter contention, and his mouth calleth for strokes.7 A fool's mouth is his destruction, and his lips are the snare of his soul.

Solomon was saying, "We have to learn to keep our mouth shut and let God do the talking." The very fact that you may be going through is the indicator that God is going to bless you. We must remain humble and keep working in silence. Let the pride go and depend on God and keep our confidence in Him. God will bless and honor us. While being quiet, we are to seek the Lord during this time.

David said, "I'm up early looking for God even though I'm out here in the wilderness where there is no water." He was out-numbered but looking for God. David was up early in the morning looking for God, expecting God to move. He was expecting God and do something for him and his people in that wilderness experience. David walked with the expectation that God was going to move on his behave. Do you expect that God is going to do something for you?

Be quiet and hide until God moves for you because He has a comeback for you. My friends keep your expectation high in God. God loves us; that's why we should have high expectation in Him. When you know that someone loves you; you know they will fight for you when things get tuff. When you know someone loves you; they won't talk about you behind your back. They will defend who you are in your absence.

You see, David had a track record with God, and he knew God loved him. He knew God made him king. He knew God had always been by his side when no one else was there. These things developed David's faith and confidence in the Lord. We to go through things, and our faith and confidence develop during trials.

David was saying, "I'm expecting to see your power and glory as I saw in the sanctuary. God can move beyond just the church, even though this where we come corporately to worship. God can move in our homes, schools, businesses, jobs, communities, and our situations. He is a great father that wants us to keep our confidence. He can deliver us in any situation because He is God.

Psalm 34:19

19 Many are the afflictions of the righteous: but the Lord delivereth him out of them all.

Psalm 119:70-73

70 Their heart is as fat as grease; but I delight in thy law.71 It is good for me that I have been afflicted; that I might learn thy statutes.72 The law of thy mouth is better unto me than thousands of gold and silver.73 Thy hands have made me and fashioned me: give me understanding, that I may learn thy commandments.

Sometimes it may not feel good, but it is good. We are learning who God can be in our lives; as we keep our confidence in Him. We're learning to hide in His Word and His ways. God loves you, and there is nothing better than God's love. It's God's love that He has for us that keeps on giving us favor and mercy.

God's love is shown to us every day when we wake up because He grants mercy. He gives us mercy to get up and do the right thing. He gives us mercy to get up and do what He has asked of us. My friends get up and make the most of the opportunities that Christ has given you! Quit talking yourself out of things that God said you could have. He loves you, and no one can change His mind towards you.

I have learned to give God praise while I wait with confidence. We must keep praising God in the good and bad times because Christ will see us through. David was saying, "I'm going to do what I would do if I were in the sanctuary." David would praise God and lift his hands to his Savior. David didn't let his wilderness experience stop his praise.

It's easy to praise God at church. We can praise God at church in front of everybody. We should be able to praise God, lift our hands when we are at home, on the road, or by ourselves. We should be able to lift our hands and our heads and give God praise. Our situations shouldn't stop us from giving Him praise because God loves us. Can we praise Him during the rainy days of our lives? When it seems like trouble always seems to find us.

Can we lift our hands and give him praise, give thanks when people are talking and have counted us out? Can we lift our hands and give him praise when the bad report comes? Can we lift our hands and give him praise when the money gets funny? Can you lift our hands and give him praise when it seems like no one will support you? We must keep our confidence in him and keep praising because trouble doesn't last always. There is an expiration date on your problem.

God has been faithful to His promises. He continues to do just what my grandmother prophesied to me and others. It is awesome to know God will never lie. I've started to pastor a church in Greensboro, North Carolina. He continues to do great work in me! I'm excited what God will continue to do in all his people. I encourage you as I close to hold on to numbers twenty-three and nineteen!

Problems have a way of coming to an end if you keep your confidence in the Lord. Problems come to an end, because God never reneges on His promises. Whatever God spoke over your life; it will come to pass. What God has for you it's done in Jesus name! We're just walking it out. I must go now but enjoy the process God has for you. He doesn't write bad checks. You can take it to the bank; your promises will happen because of what He said in numbers twenty-three and nineteen!

Tony L. Hayes

About the author

Pastor Tony Hayes (Big Slim) is from Greensboro, North Carolina. He is the pastor at Jabez Christian Center. He also the owner of a new Record label called Anointed Records. Big Slim performs, writes, and produces Gospel music. He has a passion for winning souls. He is a soul winner serving in the community. He has been preaching and teaching the Gospel for over 16 years. Tony Hayes is also a graduate of Shaw University with a degree in Religion and Philosophy. He also is a proud MC, film writer, and author declaring the Gospel. He has written a book entitled "Don't Hate Celebrate" and a stage play "The Apocalypse." He continues to represent for Christ, inspiring others along the way. Big Slim is a soldier in the Army of the Lord.

The type of music that he ministers is Gospel Hip Hop. Pastor Tony desires to influence the world with a hip-hop message of Christ in his books, films, and music. He enjoys speaking to people on issues of today that will influence their lives. God brought him out of the streets, so this is how Big Slim gives back with a positive message. Pastor Tony wants to point the youth and others in the right direction, so the music, writing, and preaching are there to educate them and let them know that there is a better way through Christ. It's about fulfilling the Great Commission.

Discography: Big Slim release his first cd Lost Son in 2004 and the hit single was Holy Ghost. He also released the LP Apocalypse in 2009. Big Slim wrote his first stage play The Apocalypse in 2010. He also released his first book "Don't Hate Celebrate in 2016. Big Slim released his new cd Hot Gospel Rhymes worldwide on 1-19-18.